~A poignant and amazing story of a woman's journey through the difficult transition from devoted wife to widow.

~Mary L. Schramski, Ph.D.,
Educator, Author

~I read your manuscript twice. Each time, your words make me feel, and eliciting emotion in one's writing is a rare gift. Your experiences in life and love are rich and your naration bring us through your stages of loss and recovery like you are a cherished friend.

~Carolyn Hayes–Uber,
President, Stephens Press

James - Thank you for buying my first book I hope you enjoy it
Beth Williams-Medher
7-28-10

The Not
So Merry
Widow

Elizabeth

Williams-Medhus

The Not So Merry Widow
Elizabeth Williams–Medhus
Copyright © June 2010
All Rights Reserved

For information about the contents of this book, or permission for reproducing portions of this book, please contact the publisher at www.mysticpublishers.com or the author at edwms@aol.com.

Library of Congress Control Number: 2010927457

ISBN: 978–1–934051–47–4

Published in the United States of America by:

Mystic Publishers

Henderson Nevada
www.mysticpublishers.com

I dedicate this book to
Edward Donald Williams, M.D., FP, MHA,
A humanitarian, a friend, a father,
my husband.

June 2, 1935 — November 22, 2005

Acknowledgements

While attending a writing class in Torrance, California, I began writing family vignettes and considered writing my memoirs. In November 2003, my husband and I moved to Sun City Anthem in Henderson, Nevada, where I joined the Anthem Authors Club and continued with the memoirs project as I received encouragement and assistance from Club members at our weekly meetings.

However, when my husband, Edward, became ill and soon died (November 22, 2005), I found it difficult to think, let alone write, about anything. I was a widow in mourning. The Club members encouraged me to continue writing and I began to pour my heart and soul onto paper, reliving the past and wondering how I would survive the future. Each week I would share my efforts with my Club friends who were very supportive. They listened and critiqued my work with compassion and caring friendship. They gave me the courage to face each day. Without their help I may not have been able to continue writing.

Mary Schramski, PhD. is an educator and a published author of many books. She is also a dear friend and neighbor who read my manuscript and said, "Beth, this is a good story and needs to be published." She offered to help with editing and selecting a publisher. Her help was invaluable but it took time for me to decide to submit my manuscript for publication.

The story sat in a drawer for a couple of years as I made attempts to go on with my life. It was then that I met Sigurd Medhus, a widower, with whom I shared many happy memories. He asked to read my story and offered to review it before submitting it for publication.

I thought I would never fall in love again, but I did. With his loving encouragement, I completed my painful journey as a widow, and now I relish each day as Elizabeth Williams–Medhus.

Table of Contents

The Not So Merry Widow

I Call Your Name
But You're Not There

"Not now Sarah," I said to my friend. "I'm not ready, maybe later. I'm just not in the mood to go out." Six weeks had passed since I had lost my husband, and I was in shock, denial, and easily became tearful.

"No, no, you come, it's a nice place, lots of nice people." Sarah is a tiny, vivacious lady who speaks with a strong Asian accent. Finally her tenacity wore me down. On a scale from one to ten, my resistance was already at a minus ten. We were to attend the weekly Saturday night dance at a Senior Citizen Center somewhere in the northern outskirts of Las Vegas.

Saturday arrived, and about four in the afternoon I thought I had better figure out what I should wear. My back was aching after playing table tennis for hours the night before, and I was beginning to procrastinate, looking for an excuse to get out of going.

Rummaging through my closet, I finally chose an attractive black and white dress suitable for a tea dance. I had no difficulty slipping into it because it had no buttons or zippers. But because of a previous back injury,

I faced the challenge of buckling my shoes with great trepidation, fearful that I might once again be left in an immobile position. Since I didn't have the flexibility of a contortionist, I knew I was in for an Advil and Bengay evening. I realized that having a husband during such times to help with zippers, buttons, and buckles was a special perk.

I started talking to Ed, my deceased husband, hoping he could hear me as my contorted body resisted my efforts. "I know you're laughing at me. Don't forget you had problems, too. Remember when a stray thread from the flap on your fly got caught in your zipper? Oh, Lord, Ed. I'm not ready for this. Sarah is like a dog with a bone. She'll nag me to death." I continued talking to thin air until finally my muscles relaxed, easing the spasm and allowing me at last to get my left shoe buckled.

When I arrived at Sarah's home, I found that she was still in a state of undress. "Oh, I am so sorry, I just got home and my husband needed his dinner before I go." She ushered me into the kitchen to meet her husband. He was in the middle of eating a rather large bowl of soup.

Before he could get up from the table, I placed my hand on his shoulder. "Please, please don't get up." He didn't. "Go on with your dinner before it cools." He did.

Since I had met him once before, I knew of his interests and we had a nice conversation until Sarah returned to the kitchen, now dressed for the evening, and suddenly it was time to leave. Plus it was Harold's poker night and he was anxious for us to leave and have his cigar–smoking buddies in for the evening.

We climbed in her sports coupe, which demanded

once again contorting my aging bones and muscles to fall into the low bucket seat. Sarah tucked the rest of my garments in next to me and made certain I was buckled in.

The Senior Center was a sparsely decorated clubhouse. I noticed a few gentlemen staring at a television in the corner of the lobby. In a room off the lobby a meeting was being held. They all stopped talking and turned to look up as we walked by. My comfort level was nonexistent. The sound of music became louder drowning out the sound of our high heels clicking on the linoleum floor. At the end of the long corridor was the main recreation room. The room was large with a highly polished wooden floor, excellent for dancing. I surveyed the room, and I saw two or three couples on the floor. One couple caught my eye. It wasn't until I blinked a few times that I realized that the man had an oxygen tank slung over his shoulder.

The lady at the door said, "That will be three dollars each, please."

My hands trembled as I fumbled through my handbag.

"No, no, you're my guest, I pay." Sarah already had six dollars ready and handed the money over.

The lady collecting the money was dressed from head to toe in dark lavender. Her shock of bleached blonde curls was held in place by a cascade of tiny purple flowers. The area around her eyes was thick with shades of lavender and her lips were painted bright red. As I covertly gave her the once over, I thought, *She must have been a very beautiful showgirl many moons ago.* In spite of all of the camouflage, she was still attractive. Her

3

smile was brilliant, warm, and inviting. If I applied all that makeup on me, I would have been mistaken for a court jester.

The beautiful lady said, "Welcome. I'm so glad you two could come because there are a few extra men tonight." *Whoopee*, I thought rather sarcastically. "Sarah, it's so good to see you again. You've brought a guest. Welcome. My name is Diane and my husband is the bandleader. Have a nice evening."

She pointed to a table where we could sit with a single, solitary male. He was easily pushing ninety. He stood and greeted us happily and introduced himself as Frank visiting from Chicago. Before I could even remove my wrap, Frank asked me to dance. Remembering my dance etiquette, I set down my handbag, removed my wrap, and accepted his offer. He was actually quite graceful. He told me that he was getting anxious since everyone else had a partner and he felt quite alone. Oh how well I knew that feeling.

During the course of the evening, a few other gentlemen asked me to dance. The second fellow I danced with, much to my chagrin, was at least a head shorter, and nice looking, with lines right out of some old movie. "Now why haven't I seen you before, Sweetheart?"

Dear Lord, help me, I pleaded silently, trying not to roll my eyes. "Well I just haven't been around before. What's your name?"

"Ron, short for Ronald," he replied. The conversation didn't get much better, but he was a fairly good dancer. "What's yours?"

"You can call me Beth, short for Elizabeth."

The third man, whom Sarah thought would make

a good dance partner for me, seemed as unenthusiastic about the prospect as I was. His body language spoke louder than words. He slouched in his seat and didn't bother to introduce himself. He was obviously uncomfortable and focused his attention on Sarah. Frank, the ninety year old, was genteel and thoughtful. At least he offered to bring me a cup of coffee.

Sarah kept reassuring me that William, the third fellow, was a very nice man. "He only wants to dance, no romancing, no girlfriends, and he is a smart dresser. He's a very, nice man, very nice."

I smiled, all the while thinking, *who is she trying to convince?* He made it obvious that he only wanted to dance with Sarah. She continued to talk as I gave William the once over. *Hmm he has no manners and as for being well dressed, I don't think so. At least he isn't sweaty, and get a load of those black and white patent leather shoes. My God, the belt is the size of a cummerbund studded with silver rivets. Oh my, my! The lavender jacket with the pink shirt and tie is way over the top.* My thoughts kept me entertained as I watched William lead her to the floor. I actually preferred having a cup of coffee with Frank. He enjoyed chatting about his family. I was able to understand most of what he was saying, despite his thick Italian accent.

Then I became conscious of a strange phenomenon. When I addressed Sarah, or one of the two men sitting at our table, that I had referred to them as Ed, my deceased husband's name. It happened over and over again. No one seemed to notice. I assumed it was either because they were hard of hearing or the music was too loud.

The dance ended at nine and Sarah decided to take me to a bar, assuring me that I would enjoy the music. Not wanting to be a wet blanket, I agreed to go. I couldn't help but remember that whenever I needed to leave the house for one reason or another, Ed would jokingly ask, "Where are you going Beth?" He knew full well that I would always answer, "I'm going to a bar and pick up some good looking boy toy and have a few drinks."

"You never go to a bar. You don't drink," he'd say.

"I went with you, silly. Remember our first date? You ordered us something called a 150. I was sick for three days. I trusted you to behave yourself and not take advantage of the situation."

"Me, never," he said mockingly. "I would never do that. I married you instead."

"I thought you married me because I was a cheap date."

I felt the gut–wrenching pangs of sorrow as I reminisced about how playful we were. Those playful moments…gone, but the memories will linger.

I went to the bar with Sarah. The musician was excellent and we did enjoy a cocktail. The place reeked of booze and smoke, causing my eyes to tear and burn. "Sarah, do you think we could leave before the next set?"

"Sure, sure, we can go. Did you have a nice time?" She was so thoughtful and wanted me to have a pleasant evening. I did try to make the most of it.

When we left the bar, the wind was howling, the air was cold and crisp. I bundled myself up in my shawl. Again, without realizing what I was saying, I blurted out, "Ed, get in the car, it's cold. You'll get sick." Sarah didn't acknowledge the fact that I had referred to her as Ed. I was stunned by the realization that no one with whom I had spoken that evening had noticed. Quizzically, I asked, "Sarah did you realize that I called you Ed? Not just now, but earlier tonight. I kept catching myself addressing everyone as Ed."

"No, but you must be thinking of him. He'll always be in your mind." How strange, no one had noticed.

Since I don't like walking into a dark, silent, empty house, I'd left the lights and radio on. I had a snack before getting ready for bed. As I climbed into bed, I took Ed's photo from the nightstand and traced his features with my finger. All I could feel was the cold glass that covered his smiling face. No longer would I feel the warmth of his arms or hear his comforting words welcoming me home. Tears rolled down my face as I whispered, "Goodnight, my love, I know you were with me tonight. Thank you for watching over me."

I lay in bed staring at the time displayed on the ceiling in bright, bold, red numbers. Seconds became minutes, and the minutes became hours. Frustrated, I started switching from one TV channel to another, hoping that I would eventually fall asleep. Sleep did not come right away. When it did, visions of the torment Ed endured came flashing back. *Ed, Ed, why you, why now?* I knew the answers, remembering our daughters talking among themselves as they packed up their father's medications.

"Mom," Carol said without looking up, "What hurts me, is that Ed knew what was happening to him. He knew what needed to be done and what was being done. He hated not being in control of his care. I can only try to imagine what emotional pain he was suffering. I feel so angry with him! I can't help the way I feel. He helped

7

so many people; why, why didn't he help himself?"

"I know, Carol, I know. I could read it in his eyes. No one ever wants to think or believe it could happen to him. Ed was like his mother in so many ways. He was a superb diagnostician, but with his own health, he had his head in the sand." I saw the silent tears well–up in the eyes of our children. The entire family knew that their father was more ill then he had let on. He was a private man and never complained. In all of the years we were married, he never missed a day of work, and seldom complained of pain. Right before he left us, he was no different.

My eyelids grew heavy; slowly I drifted off into a deep slumber, but one hour later once again I was wide–awake staring at the photo by my bedside.

"You have such a beautiful smile. Do you know that was the first thing I noticed about you when you walked into the office?"

Ed made a funny face and said, "I know, you've told me often enough."

Although he was no longer on this earth, I spoke openly as though, and maybe hoping, he could hear me. I knew what his answers would be. I repeated the time we had our first encounter. Despite his sassy remarks, I knew he liked to hear me reminisce. It was something we did every morning. We relived memories we held so dear. And for the ones not so sweet, he'd frown, look away from me, and quietly say, "Let's not talk about that."

But all my memories made me smile, as I once again began to visualize our first encounter so many years ago.

I Took One Look At You

September 29, 1965 was a typical California day, warm and sunny. I was on duty at the M.D. Medical Group in Lawndale, California. The waiting room was filled with patients, and the telephone was constantly ringing. It was not until I looked up from the appointment ledger that I noticed a young man leaning on the counter staring at me. Startled by his presence I nearly dropped the telephone. I managed to stammer, "I'll be with you shortly, Sir." He nodded and continued to smile, making me nervous.

I don't know what came over me. I became flustered. My cheeks felt as though they were on fire. *I can't be having a hot flash?* "Yes sir, I have you down to see the pediatrician on October 3rd at 3:30 p.m. Yes, his name is Dr. Williams. No, his first day will be October 3. Thank you for calling." I could hardly wait to get off the telephone. It was extremely distracting to have some stranger leaning and leering at me from across the counter.

"Hi, I have a 4:30 p.m. appointment with Dr. Bender. He'll be expecting me," the man across the counter said. Finally he shifted his position and stood erect, but he continued smiling at me. He knew he'd embarrassed me.

"Dr. Beanbaaaa, Dr. Bender is currently with a patient. May I have your name please?" I almost blew it. Dr. Bender was the primary owner of the clinic. He had a notorious reputation of being a lady's man. When he wasn't around, the staff referred to him as Beanbag.

"Yes, I'm Dr. Williams and I hear you already have patients scheduled for me. How do you know that I am going to accept the position?"

I became even more flustered. "Oh, yes we've been expecting you. No, I don't know. I just assumed…. I couldn't finish the sentence or stop my stammering. I wondered what he must be thinking of me. *He must think I'm a fool. I feel like a fool. The entire single female staff has been anxious to meet him and check him out. As for me, I hope I looked composed. I'm not, Oh Lord, I feel so embarrassed.*

Dr. Bender stopped at the desk. I made the introductions and quickly removed myself from the scene. I hurried to the restroom and leaned up against the door. My knees were knocking. I felt absolutely humiliated. I hoped Dr. Bender didn't hear me stammer; if he did, he'd never let me hear the end of it.

I didn't know what it was about that young man, Dr. Williams, but my heart was doing somersaults. There was something brash about him, and yet, I felt as though he was rather shy and vulnerable.

This memory is indelible. No matter how many times I repeated our meeting to Ed, the story never changed. Once again I turned to his photo, carrying on my one-sided conversation.

"Ed, I even remember what you wore that day. You

had on a shirt in pastel blue and yellow checks with short sleeves. You also wore contacts. I can't remember when you decided to start wearing glasses. I think it was after you married Carolee."

I was shamelessly curious about the new doctor. Later that day I retreated to the privacy of my beat up old car and noticed an even more dilapidated Volkswagen with Arkansas plates parked in the area reserved for the physicians on staff. I thought, *That can't be his car, it's in worse shape than mine.*

Driving home from work I started daydreaming about the young man. He had light brown wavy hair that was beginning to recede, soft brown eyes, and a deceptive angelic face that sported a mischievous grin. Daydreams were my escape from the reality of my marital woes. My marriage was in its final death throws. The thought of the impending divorce was frightening. After all, I had three beautiful children to support. Thoughts of returning to Canada played on my mind, yet something was pushing those thoughts aside. Little did I know that day what was in store for my children and me.

I drifted, drifted off into dreams of our yesterdays. I never bothered to wipe away the salty, remnants of tears that had dried on my cheeks.

Dreams

The sweet dreams never lasted very long.

I tossed and turned, moaning, trying to erase the vision that kept creeping into my thoughts. *Stop, please stop! This is unfair. Ed you don't deserve this torture. Why, why you? Dear God, what can I do?*

What else can a widow do except weep and mourn? The emotional ups and downs wore me out, enabling me to fall into a deep, dark sleep.

I awoke before dawn. I can't recall when I had fallen asleep; it was as though a black shroud encased my body blocking out the light, sounds, and dreams. Still groggy, I surveyed the bedroom, looking but not seeing. Throwing back the covers, I slid to the edge of the bed. I started searching for my slippers with my feet. Sliding the rest of the way off the bed, I put on my robe and lumbered out to the kitchen.

With my mind still numb, I went about my daily ritual as though nothing had happened. I filled the coffee pot, went outside for the newspapers, and set the papers on the table. I never unwrapped the papers. I left them sitting in a pile waiting to be read. Ed could never start the day without reading the daily news.

The aroma of the coffee permeated the kitchen and the alarm went off letting me know it was perked. I pulled out two mugs, the sugar, Mocha Mix, and cream. I drank my coffee black, Ed had his own formula. This was our daily ritual starting when he retired. During the thirty years prior to Ed's retirement, he always made coffee for me. While we were in the office, I called him Sir, and made his coffee. It took me one year to wean him down from four teaspoons of sugar in his coffee to one, but I could never cut back on his cream. This morning was different. I was alone.

I took my cup and sat down in the overstuffed chair in the family room. Holding the coffee mug with two hands, I kept staring up at the ceiling as though it was a movie screen and we were the performers. I didn't want my dream to end because it made me feel awake and living as though nothing had changed.

My thoughts took me back to the past, remembering the next time I saw Dr. Williams. It was October 1, 1965, his first day on the job. There was an unusual amount of hubbub going on throughout the building. It seemed as though my co-workers abandoned me and went off to welcome the new physician. I was furious.

Where did everybody go? What's going on? I couldn't believe how the female staff was reacting to the new doctor. I didn't know he was single; actually I knew very little about him.

"Dr. Cassidy, what's going on?" I asked still rather perplexed and annoyed about being abandoned.

"The gals are checking out Dr. Williams," he replied with a chuckle.

"What's so special about him?" I had my own

opinions and I wasn't going to share those thoughts with anyone.

"He's just out of the Air Force and isn't married. The way this clinic is going, it could just as well be another Peyton Place." He patted me on the back, took a chart from my hand and escorted the next patient back into his office.

The staff was a mixed bag of strange characters, ripe for an "R" rated movie. Still somewhat naive, I was getting quite an education, and it didn't take long before Dr. Williams was caught up in the social whirl of being the eligible bachelor. He was never at a loss for a date.

Weeks later he was driving a sporty, convertible, and wearing beautifully tailored suits, pastel shirts and coordinating ties. His manner became more self–assured, projecting the image of a successful physician. He was casual with the nurses and other receptionists, but with me, he was businesslike.

I interrupted my vision and asked myself, "Ed, how come you treated me like that? I wasn't putting the make on you. Everybody else was, but I wasn't. *Oh yes I would have, but who in their right mind would want a woman with three kids, two dogs, and some Chinese chickens. How many times have I heard the old saying "Never marry a woman until she has had her appendix out, teeth capped, and her own fur coat.* I thought I had probably read that saying somewhere. As for me, at that time I didn't even own a coat.

But then I remembered not too many years later Ed told me, "You were married. When I walked into that office you were the very first person I saw. I liked what I saw. Actually, I was on my way to another interview later in Long Beach. Because of you I changed my mind and decided to accept the position in the clinic.

Those were difficult years for me. The only social life I had was at work. I could barely afford to dress myself. I was working two jobs, and taking care of my neighbor's children after school. I always put the babysitting money aside so I could take my brood ice–skating at the Olympic Ice Arena in Torrance on family night. Once in a while, I had enough money to take them to a movie.

I envied the single women at the clinic. They always talked about their dates, especially when Ed had taken one of them out. Sometimes I felt so hurt because he always seemed to ignore me.

I continued on with my one–sided conversation. "One night you bought some Kentucky fried chicken and offered some to Dorothy, my supervisor who spent her time smooching with Dr.Goldstein, but you totally ignored me. I was salivating because I had never eaten Kentucky Fried Chicken and wondered what it tasted like. Ah, but later, I would get back at you. Do you remember?"

I could hear Ed's answers and see his impish expression clearly, as though he was sitting next to me.

"You won't let me forget. It amazes me that you can remember the minutest details of everything I did wrong."

This was the calm before another surge of sorrow, followed by a torrent of tears. Each day at dawn I sat alone reliving the past, trying not to think of my loss. I resented the phone calls interrupting my dreams. I neglected to call the children and our friends. I clung desperately to my solitude and memories.

I also had fond memories of one Thanksgiving Day, when I was on the late shift with Alice the nurse. Dr. Williams was on duty for twenty–four hours with little time to leave the premises for lunch or dinner. Since I had already celebrated earlier in the day with my children, I packed up leftovers to take to the clinic. Later that evening, I made a small pot of cabbage rolls to be reheated. The aroma of the sauerkraut slowly wafted down the corridor. I was sitting at the typewriter when the young doctor appeared. He leaned up against the counter and asked, "Where are all of the patients?"

I know what you're up to. Following your nose are you? I'll be damned if you can have any of my dinner.

"Mmmm, what smells so good? Have you eaten dinner yet?" Dr. Williams smiled at me as though we were buddies.

I know why you're being so friendly. Go ask your girlfriends to bring you food. You are not getting any of mine. "No, I'm just warming up some cabbage rolls I made yesterday." I answered. "Are you having fried chicken again, Dr. Williams?"

"No, I think I'll go over to the bowling alley and get something."

"Excuse me? Other doctors don't leave. Dr. Williams you're on duty this evening. What if we have an emergency?"

"There's nobody here, and you can call me."

"Dr. Williams I don't think you should leave." My tone became rather sharp.

It was obvious when he walked away that he was annoyed with me. Stopping abruptly, retracing his

17

steps, he returned and planted both hands firmly on the counter. He leaned over and said, "Do you know what's the matter with you?"

Now very annoyed, I replied "No, what?" I was being very insubordinate which shook me and my knees began to quiver.

A little red faced he replied, "You're just too damn conscientious!"

I couldn't believe I was arguing with one of my employers. I usually grumbled, but kept my opinions to myself. I was up for a pay raise. Oh, my God, Dr. Bender put him in charge of all the employees. There goes my raise. I'll be lucky if I don't get fired. I don't care. I know what I'm worth and I am not going to back down.

I don't know what possessed me. I was almost in tears. He turned and walked away when I shot back, "Since when is that a crime!"

He stopped short, but must have thought twice about responding and disappeared back to his office. I went into the kitchen to fix myself a plate and took it back to the reception desk. Alice went to check on the doctor, but his office door was closed.

"I think he's upset. What happened?"

I gave her the scenario of what we had said. Then we noticed an outside line lit up the switchboard. Almost in unison, we both blurted out "I bet he is ordering food."

Someone To Watch Over Me

Our relationship didn't seem to change. Ed was cool and businesslike and I continued as though nothing had happened. A month passed and much to the surprise of the staff, he had asked for some time off. He apparently had some unfinished business to take care of in Hawaii, where he had interned. On his return, he seemed more jovial. "Beth, would you like a donut? Just leave the chocolate–nut covered one for me. That's my favorite," he said the first day he was back.

Surprised by his offer, I meekly thanked him. My mind went blank for a moment before I could even begin to speculate about the reason for his change in attitude. But it wasn't long before I would know the answer.

Within a month Dr. Williams requested time off the first two weeks in December. Rumor had it that he would not return, but he did just prior to the annual Christmas party, walking in with his bride. A hush fell over the room. Whispers soon followed. "Boy, that was quick. Did anyone know he was getting married? No, I don't even think Leona knew." Everyone in the clinic was stunned and wondered if Leona, his former girlfriend, knew.

So that was what the unfinished business trip to Hawaii was all about. No wonder he wanted it kept a secret. I also wondered how Leola was going to take it.

I found out that Ed had known his new bride for about four months. It was a short, passionate love affair. He was lonely, and they were both trying to get over previous relationships. Ed was completely honest with me as he continued to explain, "I was engaged to a fellow medical student at Temple University. Her parents were one of the wealthier families in Philadelphia and my family didn't fit in with the socially elite. I was terribly hurt. I wanted to get as far away from Pennsylvania as I could. Carolee never said much of her past and I didn't ask. I proposed to her on my trip back to Hawaii and she accepted."

Carolee Patricia Bedard and Dr. Edward Donald Williams were married December 8th, 1965, in Duluth, Minnesota, six months after they first met. She was a Medical Records Librarian in Honolulu.

On the day of the wedding, the weather became foul; so was the mood of the bride. Many of the guests could not attend due to one of the worst blizzards of the year. Fortunately, the day before, Ed's parents, sister and brother–in–law, and his grandmother, Mary, drove approximately one thousand miles from Erie, Pennsylvania, to Duluth, Minnesota.

When Ed's family arrived in Duluth, the Bedard family was not home to receive them. The Williams family was at a loss as to what they should do next. They waited an hour in the freezing cold and decided to find the motel the Bedards had selected for them.

The reception they received was not quite what they

expected. The air was far more frigid at the reception. Binnie Bedard, the bride's mother, treated the Williams family with cold indifference upon their arrival and especially during the reception.

Ed's family used the excuse that they needed to leave early from the reception to take advantage of a break in the weather. They would rather face the challenge of racing ahead of the storm as they drove back to Erie than spend another minute being ignored.

The stormy weather on their wedding day was only the first of many marital storms that occurred during their five–year marriage, many displayed in front of staff, guests, and Ed's colleagues. It was years later that I learned that both Carolee, and Ed had been rebuffed by former lovers, and they probably married on the rebound.

The Christmas party was the first time that we would get to meet Dr. Williams' bride. Each doctor and staff greeted the couple warmly. I, too, extended my hand and offered congratulatory remarks. I was met by a pair of icy blue eyes and a limp handshake that was more of a dismissal than an acceptance. *What had I done?* But I wasn't the only employee who felt rebuffed.

The young bride, smiling, mixed and mingled with the doctors and their wives, but made a point of not mingling or even acknowledging the rest of the staff. As for me, I just couldn't understand why she seemed to resent me.

Several months passed and there were rumors that the marriage was not going well. I knew that. He was getting far too many calls from a nurse at Holly Park Hospital. It was Leola. She would end up being a thorn in his side for years.

There were many changes in the clinic. The reputation of the sexual escapades of Dr. Bender ended up costing the clinic a fortune in the loss of a major union contract. Dr. Williams decided to work for another physician in Inglewood, California. Carolee was the Medical Records Librarian at Centinela Valley Hospital, and met Dr. Harvey, a very prestigious man in the community. She wanted to be a part of the "Inner Circle." She thought if Ed was on Dr. Harvey's staff, they would be in with the socially elite. When it was announced that Dr. Williams was leaving our clinic, we were told to switch all of his patients to the remaining physicians. We were also told not to give out any information as to his whereabouts.

Fortunately, when I worked evenings, I could hear the conniving of Dr. Bender and Dr. Goldstein trying to manipulate the distribution of the profits among the other partners. I thought this was so unfair. The entire medical staff was angry and upset over the infighting of the physicians. The pyramid was crumbling.

Dr. Bender sold out to Dr. Goldstein. Dr. Goldstein brought in as office manager his knuckle–chewing brother–in–law, who drove everyone crazy, including me. I was in charge of receiving and accounting for all monies received daily in the clinic. Dr. Williams would drop by to see if any checks had come in for him. I told him the truth and said there had been several and gave him the amounts. I also told him that patients were looking for him. He gave me his new business cards and asked if I would give them to his patients should they ask. They did, and I did.

My once sanctuary of social activity was now

becoming a den of iniquity. I knew my days were numbered, so I quit. My children and I went to visit their grandparents in Canada, and we stayed with them during the spring of 1968. Upon our return, I received a message that Dr. Williams was looking for me. He had heard that I had quit. I was surprised to hear he quit the clinic in Inglewood, and was opening his own office and needed an office manager. Ed told me that he hated working in a group practice. Dr. Harvey was one of the "Good Old Boys," and spent more time on the golf course than in his office. Ed was fed up with carrying a heavier load, and not being paid accordingly.

He decided to go out on his own. Carolee, who was impressed with Dr. Harvey and his social standing in the community, knew that if her husband left the Inglewood office, they would no longer be part of the "in crowd". Their marriage became ugly, and she threatened Ed with divorce when he told her of his plans. Since Ed ignored her threats and hostile antics, Carolee realized that Ed was not going to be swayed from his plan. She eventually acquiesced. For a short period of time, civility returned to their marriage.

When Ed set up his new office he needed an office manger, and he knew I was unemployed. The office was close to his home and mine. He offered me the job and let me choose my own hours. Obviously, I needed the income and the flexibility. I accepted his offer. It didn't take long for me to realize that his two employees were taking advantage of their employer. Gretchen, the receptionist, helped herself to the office credit card, and Dina, the oversexed, medical assistant and billing clerk was not doing her job. Money was not coming in.

Fortunately, Dina quit and moved away and I caught Gretchen embezzling from insurance companies.

Our business relationship grew. Dr. Williams trusted me completely, especially after I corrected all the billings to all of the accounts, and submitted corrections and additions to the insurance companies. He finally received enough money in the following month to pay his overhead. He was pleased with the results and to show his appreciation, he invited me out to dinner. Of course, I accepted.

We were both in a state of flux with our relationships. He found out his wife was pregnant. Both of them were not pleased, since they had no intentions of having children. For the sake of the child, Ed and Carolee decided to reconcile, but only if Dr. Williams would purchase a bigger house that Carolee had already selected in Torrance, California. She threatened not to let him see his child unless he promised to purchase the house. He kept his promise

The couple grew further and further apart, no longer sharing a bed.

Their daughter, Kimberly Kate, was born July 7, 1969. I received a telephone call in the office from Carolee's mother stating, "You can tell the good doctor that he has a healthy baby girl and if he can find the time, he'll be allowed to visit."

Stunned at such a cold and heartless message, all I could say was, "He's in his office, would you like to talk to him?"

"No", she said. "Carolee specifically instructed Dr. Sylvestre and me to call Ed only after the baby was born. Just give him the message."

I didn't like being put in the position of the bearer of bad news, but I did what I had to do. By this time, when we were in private, I referred to him as Ed. "Ed, Binnie just called; Carolee is at Little Company of Mary Hospital. You have a daughter."

"Why didn't they call me sooner?" He was visibly upset. "Why didn't Dr. Sylvestre call? I can't go now; I have a patient prepped for a surgery. I'll have to go later." He checked his wristwatch; it was now two in the afternoon. "She must have been in labor before this. Why did they wait until now? They could have called earlier. Carolee knows I do hospital rounds between twelve and two. I could have been there." He stood there for a moment, too stunned to speak; then turned away from me and went into his office and slammed the door. I didn't follow.

After Carolee's mother left to return to Duluth, I received a phone call from Carolee. She'd returned to work and asked if I would consider caring for the baby until she returned from a business seminar. She also needed a full time nanny.

Carlotta was my neighbor in need of a job but would only watch the baby from Monday to Friday. Carolee was desperate to have someone watch the baby over the weekend.

"Please Beth, I have no one else to call. Carlotta said she could take Kimmy over to you on Friday, and I'll pick her up on Monday." Carolee was persistent, "It would only be for the weekend."

"I don't know. Why can't Ed take care of her? He's not on call this weekend."

"No, I don't want him left alone with my daughter.

Please Beth, I need a favor."

Against my better judgment, if I had any, I couldn't say no. It was not just Carolee's child but Ed's as well.

Before she left we got together and she went over her instructions. I still had a crib in storage, so the baby would be perfectly comfortable and safe from my two dachshunds. George loved children, but Max couldn't be bothered; he loved George.

During Carolee's visit, we had a long, intimate conversation. She asked why I was divorced. I told her the truth, except for the fact that I was in love with her husband. She told me about her past, and she knew that she and Ed were not suited to each other. In fact, she stated, "If anyone should be married to Ed, it should have been somebody like you. I was in love with an editor of a newspaper in Honolulu. Unfortunately his wife was dying of cancer and he wanted me to wait, but I couldn't. I knew she could linger. I wanted him now, not years later. As for Ed, did you know he was engaged?"

"No, I didn't, but I knew he was serious about a nurse in L.A." Her face twisted into a sour look, as though she was sucking on a lemon.

"Yah, I know about that one, too. No, his fiancée was the daughter of one of the V.P.'s of Anchor Hocking Glass, and the parents did not approve of Ed's family. They felt their daughter was marrying below her social status. That's when Ed and I met."

"You must have loved him?"

"I thought I did at the time, but I am not in love with him now."

"Carolee, can I ask you a question?"

"Sure," she replied.

"When we first met, you were so cold and indifferent to me. Why, what set you off?"

She laughed. "Oh, I remember. You had a funny accent, and I thought you were putting it on. You still have a funny accent. I didn't know you were from Canada."

I chuckled. "My mother complains that I talk like a Yankee and speak too fast. She keeps telling me to slow down. I thought by now I would have lost my accent."

Despite the congenial conversation, my guts were twisting painfully. I was feeling cheap and dishonest. I didn't know what I should do. I kept my distance from Ed, but in the tight quarters of our working space, our longing for each other only increased. I could hardly look at the man without tears welling up. I always looked down, mumbling whatever I had to tell him.

The following Friday after I arrived home from work, Carlotta, the nanny, brought over three–month old Kimberly Kate. She had chubby cheeks, a peaches–and–cream complexion and blond fuzz on the top of her head. She had her mother's pale blue eyes, her father's round face, and there was no denying she was Ed's child. My children gathered around tickling her chin and cooing. My youngest son, Robert, who we called Bobby, would not leave her side, nor did George, the dog.

Over the next several months, Kimberly bonded with Robert. Her first words were "Baba." Every time her mother or Carlotta came to pick her up after being away, Kimberly would scream and flail her arms about, then stretch them out toward Robert, calling, "Baba, Baba."

"What is Kim trying to say?" Carolee asked, annoyed and frustrated at her daughter's antics.

"She's calling out to Bobby." I replied quietly.

"No!" she exclaimed angrily. "She's saying Mama!"

Carolee left in a huff, loaded down with a diaper bag and a screaming infant. I did not help or follow her out to the car. I knew she was upset and this would become a bone of contention between us.

Carolee was gone most of the time, enhancing her career. She left her daughter in the care of others. The child continued to bond with my children, especially with Robert who hovered over her. There is no doubt in my mind that Carolee loved her child, and showered her with as much love and affection as any other mother would, but she always said that she was not intended for "motherhood."

In March of 1971, before her thirty–second birthday, Carolee died from a rare heart condition brought on by an electrolyte disturbance due to an evening of heavy drinking and years of chain smoking. A memorial service was held in California, and Ed returned her remains to the Bedard family plot in Duluth, Minnesota.

Little did we know that the only memory Kimberly would have of her mother was of Kim pointing to cigarettes at the checkout counter in the market, and calling, "Mama".

Once I Had A Secret Love

The humidity was high and I was feeling rather lethargic when I received a letter addressed to me at the office. It was from my attorney stating that the final hearing on my divorce case was scheduled for September 27, 1971. The month and day were the same as the day I was first married. I wondered if this was an omen or just a coincidence.

My stomach went into turmoil, and I was nauseated because I was frightened, not only for myself, but also for the welfare of my children. I sat slumped in my chair at the office, reading and rereading the letter.

I felt Ed's hands on my shoulder as he knelt down beside me. Whispering in my ear, he said, "I'll go with you."

Sobbing, I said, "You can't. You have a full schedule of patients."

"I've already asked Karen to reschedule for the next day. I'm going with you."

Days later when the children were in school, Ed picked me up at my home. We rode in silence all the way to the Los Angeles Court House. After he parked the car, I looked at him and asked, "Are you coming in with me?"

"No, I'll wait here for you. It'll be better that way."

I walked slowly down the terrazzo corridor and sat outside the assigned courtroom. Every footstep echoed. The echo stopped when I took a seat.

"Beth, we need to go over a few things before we step inside the courtroom," my attorney explained. "The more we settle here, the quicker the proceedings will go."

I never looked up, but I heard every word my attorney said. My soon–to–be ex–husband and his attorney arrived at about the same time. After a few heated exchanges, we agreed on the terms and entered the room where we received the final divorce decree. I felt as though a thousand pounds had been lifted from my shoulders. I was ecstatic. I raced down the corridor, and down the steps of the courthouse, running as fast as I could to the parking lot. Ed was still there, waiting for me as he had promised. He saw me coming and got out of the car. I flew into his arms and he held me close; then we drove back in silence to his office.

The outer office was vacant and we went into the inner office. Ed sat in his chair, and I curled up on his couch. "Are you hungry?" he asked.

"No, I'm just exhausted. I feel free and yet I feel sad. I knew I had made a terrible mistake on my wedding day, but I was only nineteen, and I thought I could change the world; obviously I couldn't. William and I were like oil and water. He had a tough life sitting in Displaced Person camps after World War II. At age fifteen, he was thrown in with the good, the bad and the ugly. He's the kind of man who should have never married and had children."

Ed listened as I talked on and on. The next thing I knew he was calling me, "Beth, Beth, wake up."

"I must have drifted off. I remember talking to you. How long did I sleep?"

"Come on, get up, I'm taking you home, the kids will be coming home from school and you need to be there for them."

We were now free to openly date, but we kept our affair private. We never attended any event without taking along his office staff, as he had done before. He and I both felt, out of respect for his deceased wife, a year of mourning should be observed. The months slipped by and our love for each other grew in so many ways. It is difficult to express the love and respect we had for each other. We had no doubts about our relationship until his colleagues began to prod him into sharing their little black address books.

Dr. Alan Taylor talked openly to Ed in front of me as though I wasn't there. He told Ed about a model and claimed he'd set him up with a date. I could feel the heat rise in my veins, spewing steam through my ears. Dr. Taylor happened to glance over at me and shrank back. I glared at him with eyes that would pierce his thick skin. If he didn't see me before, he certainly did that day. Years later, he mentioned to me that he had never experienced such a forceful, telling stare.

"If looks could kill, I would have been dead. I didn't know that you and Ed were serious about one another."

What a jerk. If only he knew what I was thinking.

Dr. Kissel, my former employer, although he liked and respected me, encouraged Ed not to get serious with anyone. He felt it was too soon. Little did he know just how serious we were. I suppose all of Ed's buddies were feeding him lines about not getting married, and kept pushing names of potential dates on him. Even his old girlfriend Leona came back into the equation.

Love Me Or Leave Me

The problems in Ed's life came to a head when he had to hire a nanny to care for the baby full time. He awoke one Saturday morning and found that the nanny had disappeared during the night, taking a few valuables with her and leaving him and the baby alone.

I received a call Sunday morning asking for help. Ed didn't know what to do or who to call. I was already managing his office and helping him care for Kimberly on weekends along with my own brood. Carlotta was willing to continue caring for the baby during the day, but refused to care for her at night. I was becoming worn, weary, and depressed. I felt worthless. I suppose every divorced person goes through that feeling of rejection. A married woman looks at a divorcee as a threat, good friends no longer invited me to parties or family affairs, and some men thought I was in need of sexual gratification and nothing more.

After a lot of thought, I packed up my children and went over to help Ed. One day we were having a picnic out by the pool when he received a phone call. I knew something was amiss when his voice changed an octave and he went into the house. A bit later he came out of the house and asked if I could stay at the house. He said something had come up and he wasn't certain when he would be back. *I knew it.* I felt it. It was written all over his face. He had been invited out on a date.

"Ed, I have no problem taking care of Kimberly, but if you think I am going to allow you to use me as your chief cook and bottle washer, well think again!"

I was already feeling rejected by society, and I certainly could not take this from the man I loved and I thought loved me. I ran out of the house sobbing and climbed into my car. He ran after me, yelling for me to stop.

"Beth, stop, stop." He tried to open the door, but I had locked it.

"What will I do with the kids? You can't leave."

I gunned the engine, burned rubber, and pulled out of the driveway, leaving him standing alone. I didn't know where I was going. I found myself in a daze driving up Normandie Avenue near Redondo Beach Boulevard.

Glenna lives near here, I need someone to talk to. I feel rotten. Glenna and I had become good friends when she worked as a nurse at Hawthorne Memorial Hospital. She also was recently divorced, and sometimes we commiserated.

I knocked on her apartment door. When she opened the door, I started sobbing.

"Beth, what's wrong, what happened?" She acted genuinely concerned.

"Glenna, I can't live like this. I can't stand it anymore. I feel as though Ed is taking me for granted. I just can't do it anymore. I need to take my children home, back to my parents. There is no way in Hell that I will raise my children like this."

"You need a drink."

"No, I don't drink, it makes me sick. Well … on second thought, yes, I think I do need a drink. Maybe, when I wake up this nightmare will be over."

I drank a shot of vodka and then another. My head started to spin and I started crying again. I don't know if I had a third or a fourth shot but I know I had more than I had had in my lifetime.

"I think you better lie down. I'm calling Ed."

"No, don't." Slurring my words, I protested. "He doesn't care. All he wants is a housekeeper while he goes out with his floozy girlfriends who never give a damn about him. He can have them. They probably never changed a shitty diaper in their lives. Oh, I feel woozy."

The alcohol did its job and I must have passed out or fallen into a deep sleep. All I know is that I woke up in Ed's bed.

"Mommy, Mommy, are you okay?"

I opened my eyes and saw three pairs of eyes starring at me.

"Where am I?" I was still groggy and disoriented from the vodka.

"Its okay, Mommy. We slept here. Dr. Williams is taking us to school. It's okay Mommy, everything is going to be okay." I can't recall who said it, but it was probably my eldest son, Les, because he was twelve.

Out of the mouth of babes … My children were concerned for me; concerned for a mother who left them, got drunk and lay in a stupor. I didn't want my children to see me like this ever again. I felt ashamed and I cried, not for me, but for

35

them.

Ed took the children to school and the baby to Carlotta's house. I stayed in bed. I couldn't get up. My head felt as though it was twice the size of my body and weighed as much. It was a horrid sensation. *I'm going to die. What's wrong with me I can't move? God help me, I'm so sick.*

I heard footsteps coming down the hallway. It was Ed. I pulled the bed covers over my head and buried my face in the pillows.

"I'm back, and we need to talk."

I couldn't look at Ed; I was ashamed, angry, and terribly hurt.

"I don't want to talk to you. I've made up my mind. We won't be in your way anymore. I'm going home." I could barely talk, and my mouth felt as though it was stuffed with dirty cotton socks. *I should have stuffed my mouth with candy instead, at least I would have enjoyed the taste and I wouldn't be so damned hung over.*

Ed sat on the edge of the bed and said calmly, "You are home."

My mouth was puckering as I fought back the nausea. "No, I'm not. I don't have a home. I have to sell my house. My children won't have a home here. I need to go back to Canada." I began perspiring profusely. The vile taste in my throat and mouth intensified. Moaning, I cried out, "I'm dying. I'm going to be sick. Help me, I'm going to throw up."

"You're not dying you're just hung over."

Exasperated, Ed pulled me up off the bed. He threw one of my arms around his neck and held me around my waist while I walked limply into the bathroom. Kneeling next to the toilet, Ed rubbed my back as I wretched and gagged, trying to rid my body of the alcohol. I held my head deep into the cavity of the bowl. That was enough to make a sober person want to vomit. *Beth, you fool, you. I am never going to touch that stuff ever again. How can anyone drink?* Horrible sounds echoed in my ears from the painful contractions as I vomited.

Finally, relieved and somewhat more coherent, Ed wiped my face and helped me back into bed. He returned within a few minutes and gave me a shot of compazine to quell the nausea. I was not too numb to yelp at the rather sharp jab in my butt. *I bet he did that on purpose.*

"We'll talk when you're feeling better."

I slept and I did feel somewhat better, but I still could not get up without falling over. Later Ed came in to see if I was still sleeping.

"I'm awake. I need to go home." I didn't lift my head, nor did I move.

"Do you feel like talking?" He sounded concerned.

"I think so. We might as well get it over with. I can't take anymore of this torture."

"I want to marry you." He spoke softly, "I love you, Beth, I do."

Did I hear what he said? Am I hallucinating? Did he ask me to marry him?

"I don't know what to say or how to tell you. But I'm afraid of getting married again. Carolee and I," he paused and climbed onto the bed. I felt his arm around my waist pulling me closer to him.

Ed continued to explain his feelings. "Our marriage was a nightmare. There's so much I haven't told you, and I don't want to."

37

My head was clearing rapidly. I knew how difficult it was for Ed to talk about his past, and now he was bearing his soul and I listened until he was finished.

"Ed, do you love me because you need me? I'm not Carolee. It's not fair of you to compare us. I don't compare you to William. You know how I feel about you. You've always trusted me with everything you have, especially your daughter. I know you're afraid. The two of you never wanted children. I can understand that you're taking a risk marrying a woman with three children, but I can't take any risks with the lives of my children, either."

My tone was more adamant. Six lives were at stake. Neither Ed nor I could afford to make a mistake. "If you marry me, you marry my children as well. They'll be your children and not stepchildren; your child is my child. If you can't accept this, then I can't marry you."

He tightened his grip and pulled me closer. We sat huddled in silence thinking of what we had talked about.

Finally, he broke the silence. "I need you because I love you. Let's get married."

"Do you mean it, I mean do you really mean it? You're not just pacifying me are you?" I was still skeptical about his abrupt proposal so I thought I would put him to the test. "We need to set a date. What about May 31st?"

"No, that's a little soon. What about September?"

"Do you have more doubts? Ed, don't play games with me."

"I'm not, but…"

I pulled away from his grasp, sat upright and turned toward him. "But what?" I asked. Trying to control my emotions, I countered calmly, "Okay, let's compromise, how about July 29th?"

"I've been wanting to buy you an engagement ring, but I didn't know if you would want a diamond or might consider having a set of matching wedding bands done in Lapis?"

Boy, he thinks fast. I bet he's been thinking about proposing. Men always need to be prodded into making up their minds. I thought for a moment, and then responded with great enthusiasm. "Yes, yes, I really like the idea of matching bands. We could have the jeweler at Star of Siam design the bands."

We were married in the living room of his home in Torrance, California on July 29, 1972. Reverend Buskirk, Ed's pastor from Erie, Pennsylvania, officiated. Surrounded by our closest friends and family we exchanged our vows, "Till death do us part." Dr. Kissel, Ed's colleague, stood in for my father. Glenna and my cousin, Gabor, were witnesses. Two of the children, Carol and Leslie, stood beside us, while our youngest son, Robert, searched for the two Lapis Lazuli gold wedding bands he had dropped. During the service, Kimberly fell asleep in a little chair next to the fireplace. No sooner had we exchanged rings, then the dogs, Max and George, began howling at the fire engine sirens wailing in the distance. Startled out of a sound sleep, Kimberly added to the bedlam, shrieking. I swear I even heard church bells peel.

We were finally married. *Welcome to the real world, Ed, and you said you didn't want children.* I could only smile at the thoughts that kept going through my mind. *I wish I could've read his mind when he said, "I do." Oh, what a life we've had, if only…*

The telephone rang and startled me. Reluctant to break away from my memories, I slowly picked up the receiver. It was Les.

"Mom, how are you today?

"I'm okay, Son. Mornings are very difficult for me. I do better during the day." My voice started to break and I told myself to keep my composure. The kids had their own set of problems and I didn't want to burden them with mine. "What's up? By the way, did you hear anything from Kari?"

"Mom, does life get any easier?

"Nope." I knew something was bothering him. He needed to talk, and I needed to listen. "Son, life is a bumpy road, so enjoy the smooth ride and prepare for the pot holes."

"Wow, you didn't have to put it so strongly. I received a bill for four thousand dollars from the emergency room for Kari. No one bothered to let me know she was sick. His problems took my mind off of mine. All I could do was offer a suggestion or two. When we hung up I felt as though my pothole just got deeper but I needed to follow my own advice.

My God, will these heartaches ever cease. I don't know how we got through raising four kids without losing one. Now it's grandkids. I don't know if I could handle the loss of a child, losing my husband is … I don't know how I can stand this … Dear God. Why, why did you take him so soon? Couldn't you wait just a bit longer?

I wish I hadn't picked up the telephone. Now I have to put into practice what I had just preached to Les … and try to find the road with the fewest potholes.

July 29, 1972

The Last Dance

Monday, November 1, 2005, Ed and I always went to our dance class. He once had taught ballroom dancing when he was in college. Although the two strokes he had affected his balance, we still continued. It broke my heart to see him struggle. I remembered the days when we would glide across the floor as he held me close. He would often make silly faces at me, crossing his eyes as we danced to the seductive rhythm of the Bolero. He knew it annoyed me, and I would then pull his face towards me and kiss him on the tip of his nose, crossing my eyes as well.

I didn't notice anything different about Ed that evening at our dance class; he seemed fine except for a chronic cough, which was more of a tickle in his throat than a cough. "Are you okay?" I asked.

"It's the desert air." Ed seldom complained.

"Are you being honest with me? It sounds like you have something caught in your throat and you're trying to clear it."

Agitated at my constant questioning, he replied sharply, "I'm okay, let's go home."

Tuesday, November 2, 2005, we went about our daily

routine, I to my writing session and Ed to the gym. I returned home about 3:45 p.m. Ed wasn't home.

I was on the telephone catching up with calls when I heard Ed come in through the garage. He always sang out to me, "I'm home," but this time he just waved at me and went into the bedroom. The sun was setting, and I had my back to the living room still chatting on the telephone. Finally I finished with my calls, and as I was putting the phone back into the charger, I heard Ed call.

"Beth, help me up."

Swinging my chair around I looked in the direction of Ed's voice. At first I didn't see him in the darkened room. When I finally did, fear swept over me and I froze in the chair. He lay helpless on the floor, vainly trying to get up.

"Beth, help me up."

I leapt from the chair and, when I reached down to help him, he felt damp, cold, and clammy.

"Ed, what happened?"

"My knees went weak; I think I stumbled on the carpet. I can't get up."

"Why didn't you call sooner?" I was shaking and tried with all my might to help him up, but I couldn't. "I'm calling the neighbors. We need help."

"No, no, just get the stool."

I did as he asked, and we both struggled. I was frantic. My lip quivered as I tried to hold back a nervous laugh. "Ed, I'm calling Kathy and Jim, she's a therapist and knows the proper way to help you." He said nothing.

No sooner had I put the telephone down, then our neighbors arrived and helped pick Ed off the floor.

"Just help me to the bedroom." His voice was calm, but I could tell by his facial expressions, he was diagnosing himself.

I was on the phone again, calling our doctor, when Kathy came back and told me she didn't think this was an ordinary fall. We both thought Ed might have had a heart attack or another stroke. I was still by the phone, when I heard Ed call out.

"Kathy, tell Beth to call 911. I won't make it to the doctor's office."

I immediately called 911, and then called the doctor back to inform him that Ed would be going to St. Rose Hospital. Jim and Kathy stayed by his side, as I collected his medications, medical records, and things he would need while in the hospital. I felt like a robot moving automatically from one chore to another.

The paramedics arrived in minutes. The room filled with equipment, and at least six paramedics took their positions in administering oxygen, checking blood pressure, and drawing blood. One medic took me aside.

"Why wasn't this man in the hospital yesterday?" he asked abruptly.

Upset at his tone, I could only reply, "He had no symptoms yesterday, this just happened. When I went to pick him up, I could hear the crackling in his chest. The only symptom I could see or hear, and had previously questioned him about, was his chronic cough. He kept telling me it was caused by the desert air."

"He's a very sick man, as soon as we can stabilize him, we'll be on our way to the hospital. You can ride up front." His voice softened a bit, apologetic after almost accusing me of neglect.

I didn't know what to do. I felt as though my body was made of quivering jelly. I was lost in a mental whirl of searching, for what I don't know. I was losing control. Kathy tried to keep me on track by talking softly and giving me instructions.

I climbed into the ambulance and heard Ed answering questions. I was so nervous. I talked nonstop. I kept telling the driver what a wonderful man he is and I went over and over his medical history. The driver just nodded and let me ramble.

Ed went through a preliminary examination in the hospital: blood work, x–rays and scans. He seemed to be settling down. The crackling in his chest was fading.

The doctor came in and said that Ed was suffering from flash pulmonary edema and congestive heart failure. He told us that as soon as a bed was available my husband would be admitted to the Intensive Care Unit. I stayed with Ed and we chatted. He never discussed his condition or even tried to speculate about what triggered the edema. We were both frightened, but didn't want the other to see the fear. I knew he would be in the hospital for a day or two after the complete gamut of diagnostics tests. I kissed him good night and told him I would be back in the morning.

The next morning I visited him in Intensive Care and he was improving nicely. The nurse advised me that he would be moved to the medical floor later in the day. I left the hospital after lunch and told Ed that since he was stable, I probably would not be back till the next morning. The children were coming in from California and I had to pick them up at the airport. He was calm, his color was good, and he was no longer wheezing.

But I couldn't stay away; I went back to the hospital at 4:30 p.m. He had been transferred and was sitting up in bed.

"Wow, you're not hooked up to anything." I was elated. "Who brought you the roses?"

"Kathy Baird came by. I thought you weren't coming back." He smiled and I knew he was happy to see me.

"You know me, I can't resist you. I get so lost rambling around the house without your being there. Move over." I climbed into bed with him. He rolled over and I snuggled up close, placing my head on his back. It felt so good to feel his warmth, until…I heard a low crackle. I listened carefully. The crackling intensified.

"Did you hear that? Beth, did you hear? Ring for the nurse. I need to get some Lasix. I'm getting uncomfortable."

"Ed, I'm ringing, but no one is coming. I'll go get a nurse." A nurse just happened to be walking by and I asked her to get my husband an injection of Lasix.

"He has no orders, I have to call the doctor." She kept on walking as I walked alongside explaining that he knew exactly what he needed. "He just came from Intensive Care, there should be orders, why are there no orders? He's a physician, he knows there are orders."

Unable to ignore my pleading, she said, "I'll check."

Returning to the room I told Ed the nurse was going to call for orders. The crackling was increasing. "Help me up," Ed said. I helped Ed into a sitting position with his feet dangling over edge of the bed.

"Get the nurse." He could hardly talk.

A young aid tried placing an oxygen cone over his face, but he barked at her that it wasn't what he needed and he yanked it off his face. He was now laboring, fighting for every breath.

Again, I ran after the nurse, who seemed to be doing nothing other than walking up and down the corridor. "Damn it, my husband is in distress, and he needs help now!" I cornered the nurse just outside his door, and as we both turned to enter, Ed's eyes rolled up into his lids and he fell back. "Oh, my God, Ed, Ed." I was screaming as I ran to his side. "Ed, hang on, hang on!"

I was pushed aside and heard, "Get her out of here." Still holding his hand, I kept pleading with him to hold on. Within seconds the crash cart was moved into the room and an army of medical staff was pounding on his chest and ramming a tube down his throat. Blood splattered out of the tube and onto the linens. I felt helpless and sobbed uncontrollably as I was shoved out of the room.

"Stay with her, and don't leave her side." I had no idea who was saying what. I buried my head in my hands and tried to pray.

Grabbing the nurse by her arm I said, "I kept pushing the call button, no one came. Why were there no orders for a diuretic? He was admitted with congestive heart failure and pulmonary edema. It's routine to forward orders." I was frustrated. I knew that orders were always sent with patients for continuity. Surely some orders were sent from ICU. Adding insult to injury, he was not on any monitor, nor was his call button plugged into the electrical outlet.

Her only response was, "It looks like someone forgot to plug it in."

I was told to sit in the waiting room outside of CCU

until they had him settled. The nurse disappeared, I was kept away from the man I loved, and I cannot explain the helplessness I felt. The tears began to extinguish the fire that raged within me.

Our eldest son Les was with me when we were able to go into his room. Ed's gown, and bed linens were still bloody and had not been changed. Les went to the nurse attending Ed and demanded that they remove the damp, bloody clothing and bedding.

"We've ordered a special bed for your father. It's best that we wait until then." Her voice was soothing and her answers made sense.

Les accepted what the nurse said, but I could see the anger and concern on his face. His lips were tight and he was grinding his teeth.

This time I could not crawl onto the bed and hold him close. The bed rails were up and I counted at least eight different intravenous lines filling every orifice. He could not speak. His soft brown eyes reflected his uncertainty about the future.

I thought back to the first time he was hospitalized thirty years ago. He was in total control of his care. He exuded complete confidence in his surgeon, as well as his prognosis. But this hospitalization, thirty years later, showed his vulnerability. He was now in the hands of complete strangers.

Yesterday When I Was Young

During the sixties and until his retirement December 31, 2000, he was always in good health, with the exception of a few minor ailments. Ed was a well–respected physician in the South Bay and was Chief of Staff at Robert F. Kennedy Medical Center. He was different from most of the physicians I had worked with over the years, Ed never had an ego issue. He was always respectful to everyone. He didn't judge individuals by their lot in life, but what he or she contributed to humanity. It was no wonder he was named the City of Lawndale's 'Man of the Year,' not once, but twice. During the thirty plus years we were married, he was seldom ill. He never complained and only missed tending to patients for one week because of surgery for an inguinal hernia.

One day while I was preparing dinner for the family, Ed came into the kitchen and started lifting pot lids. He wasn't his usual self. He didn't comment on what I was cooking but asked, "Beth, do you remember when I carried you over the threshold of our honeymoon hotel?"

"Yes." I laughed. "What made you think of that? You couldn't get my other leg up and got tangled up in my dress. Gabor and Glenna were laughing and made us laugh, and you finally half carried and half dragged me into the room. Come to think of it, you just dumped me onto the bed. We were laughing so hard; all four of us fell on the bed. It's a wonder the bed didn't collapse." I took the pot lid out of his hand and shooed him away from the stove.

"I need to have a hernia repaired"

"What! Don't you dare say I'm the cause of your hernia. I wasn't that heavy. It's probably congenital." That was the first time he ever complained of pain, although there were times when I saw him wince and discreetly place pressure on his groin.

He scheduled his surgery with Dr. Kissel. The day of the surgery I drove Ed to the hospital, but not before he checked in at the office to make certain that the staff was taking care of his patients. The hospital was across the street and I walked over with him. Ed walked into the admitting office, admitted himself by filling out his history and physical documents. He wrote out the appropriate medical orders for pre–op and post–op, as well as orders for lab tests and x–rays.

"When do you think you're going to your room? You're the patient you know." I was rather amused but impressed with his air of confidence and manner. It was as though he was admitting someone else. The only difference was that he wanted me with him. He was reading his chest x–ray when he heard a page.

"Dr. Williams, please report to admitting." He picked up the phone and said he would be right out. Finally, in the middle of the corridor an orderly caught up with him and suggested he needed to go to his room, get undressed and into bed. He obliged. Once in bed, I could tell he was getting a little nervous. For once, I couldn't get a word in edgewise because he chattered on and on.

"Mrs. Williams," the orderly said, "I need to prep Dr. Williams, and give him his pre–op injection. Would you mind leaving for a few minutes?"

"Of course not. Are you going to give him a bikini wax or just a plain old shave job?" I gave Ed a wink. "You know, I could have done that for you at home."

Ed turned beet red, and gave me that, "knock it off" look. He was embarrassed. I was snickering as I drew the drape around his bed. I was on the other side of the drape, listening to his nonsensical dialogue with the orderly. I knew the injection was beginning to take effect. Moments later a 'Code Blue' was called.

"I need to go. It's an emergency." Ed said as he pushed off his covers.

"Where do you think you're going?" I asked.

"It's a Code Blue, any physician in the hospital must respond."

"Ed, for God's sake, you're not a physician now, you're a patient. What would the patient think if he saw you coming in with your gown flapping in the breeze, to administer CPR? If the patient isn't having a heart attack now, he certainly will after he gets a load of you."

Fortunately, the orderly and nurse arrived and shifted Ed onto a gurney. They pulled up the rails and started wheeling him down through the corridor to the operating room. I walked along side holding his hand while he kept insisting he must answer the Code Blue. By the time we reached the O.R., he was in dreamland.

I kissed him on the forehead and reassured him that I would be close by on the other side of the doors. He gave me a sleepy nod.

The surgery went well, and he recovered quickly from the anesthetic. He slept off and on during the day and I went home in the evening. The next morning, I received a telephone call at 6:30 a.m. Before I could even complete a sleepy hello, Ed said, "Come and get me. I've already completed the discharge orders."

"Ed, what are you talking about, you just had surgery yesterday." I was stunned.

He wouldn't take no for an answer. Not only didn't he take no for an answer, before we left for home he insisted that we stop by the office.

Dr. Newman was using our office temporarily, since his own office was still under construction. In the meantime, he would take care of Ed's patients during his recuperation. Dr. Newman was notorious for always being extremely late. This morning was no different. The waiting room was filled with patients. Ed took one look and started barking orders at the staff to get the first patient in a room. He was furious.

"Where the hell is Dr. Newman? Call the hospital and see when he'll be here?"

"Ed, stop, I'm taking you home. You've just had surgery. They're Dr. Newman's orthopedic patients, not yours. Just get in the damn car. I'm taking you home."

Still grumbling, and probably beginning to feel a little pain, he acquiesced and followed me out to the car. "You didn't have to snap at me. I could have taken care of those patients."

"I didn't snap at you, I just raised my voice a little.

You know you're being very foolish. I opened the passenger door, but he didn't get in.

"I think I'll sit in the back, I'm not feeling so good." He climbed in and was quiet all the way home.

During his recuperation, he rested, read, and talked. "You know, Beth, I was just thinking how a patient must feel facing surgery, probably scared, not knowing what's going to happen. I have to admit, I was frightened."

"Well now you can share your experience with them, maybe even show them your scar." I was making light of his observation. "Your patients trust you, especially since they know we use the same physicians, to whom we refer, for our own family. That says a lot, Ed." He put his head back on the sofa and continued pondering about patient reactions to hospitalization, then mumbled aloud, "I think I'll write a paper about it."

As Long As He Needs Me

Ed's last two hospitalizations in 2002 were brief and his prognosis was fair to good. But this time … this time was serious. He was now in the Critical Care unit. I called the family and their response was immediate. I don't know what I would have done without our children. We alternated visits with Ed. Our eyes were always watching the monitors, reading his respiration, blood pressure, and heart beats. When he was feeling perky, we would joke with him. Robert made up a signboard so he could point or try to spell words. Carol asked if he would like a puppy when he came home. He nodded and put up two fingers.

"You want two puppies?" Carol asked.

His eyes lit up and he gave a vigorous nod.

"I suppose you want a male and female?" Again he nodded.

"Black and tan, or red?"

He tried saying something and put up one finger.

"Oh, you want a pair of black and tan pups."

Again he responded enthusiastically. We were elated and encouraged by his actions. It gave us hope. The nurse finally came in and told us we were taxing the patient and we needed to let him rest.

Each day brought on new emotions. Infection set in and he was running a temperature, and probably fighting pneumonia. He took baby steps forward and major steps backward. We were in limbo. Each day we questioned the doctors and, basically received the same answers, "We need to control his temperature, we need to control his blood pressure," and so on. Still, we all put up a good front and Ed probably put up the biggest front of all. The entire family was filled with a million questions. The rhythm of the pendulum was out of balance, and we never knew which way the pendulum was going to swing.

Twelve days later, on a Monday night, I left the hospital around eleven in the evening. I pulled out of the parking lot and for the first time, I started falling apart. I couldn't see to drive. Blinded by tears, I pulled over to the curb and called home on my cell. Les answered the phone.

Crying uncontrollably and not waiting for Les to answer, I hiccuped, "I'm not coming home, I'm going to a bar."

Stunned, he couldn't believe what he had heard, "What did you say?" Then I heard him holler, "Kim, Mom just said she's going to a bar!"

"What? She never goes to bars." I could hear her voice echoing in the background.

"You don't drink. Mom, where are you going, which bar?" Both were asking questions at the same time.

"I...I...I... don't know." Trying to control the sobbing, I blurted out the only bar I knew. "Trumpets, I'm going to Trumpets."

"Mom, go to Trumpets. Kim and I will meet you there." Then he hung up.

I don't know how I got to Anthem Center, but I remember getting stuck in the revolving doors. Finally the doors began to move. I was frustrated, confused, and agitated. The place was empty except for a lady sitting at the reception desk. Bewildered I asked, "Where is everyone? Why isn't the bar open?"

Concerned at the sight of an agitated female, the lady responded, "No, it's closed on Monday. May I help you?"

I slumped down in a chair in front of her and began to survey the surroundings. Annoyed with myself, I finally responded, "The one time I want to go to a bar, the damn thing is closed."

"Are you all right, is something wrong?" The receptionist was genuinely concerned and rightfully so. I must have looked like a wreck. For all she knew I could be an escapee from the mental ward.

"My husband is in the hospital and I don't know what is happening. I'm falling apart. I'm sorry. I just can't stop crying." I poured my heart out to the lady and she listened.

She started talking to me about her loss, and then Les and Kimberly came rushing through the doors.

"Mom, we're taking you home." Without waiting for my answer, my son and daughter lifted me out of the chair as though I was a rag doll and started walking me toward the door. "How about some hot tea with lemon juice, just the way you make it for us when we're not feeling well?" Kim asked.

Numbed by fear and not knowing what the next

day would bring, I responded weakly, "Yes, that would be nice. Take me home. I want to go home." I turned and looked back over my shoulder at the receptionist, "Thank you for talking with me, thank you."

The lady gave a melancholy smile and watched as the three of us challenged the revolving door.

I called Ed's family early the next morning and told them that maybe they should come. Ed's mother, Sophie, sister Nancy, and Nancy's husband, Bob, flew in from Erie, Pennsylvania. The pulmonologist had removed the intubation tube from Ed's throat, and he was able to say a few croaky words. Although his throat was raw, he felt more comfortable.

When his mother walked into the room, she asked, "How are you feeling, Ed?"

"Marvelous, just marvelous."

I heard myself laugh at his sarcastic response. I was elated. I could have jumped through hoops. For the first time, I had hope, real hope that he would come home. My heart was pumping as I clenched my fists to my lips trying to control the hysteria in my voice. I needed to be in control; I wanted Ed to see that I had every hope in the world that he would come home.

I left the family so that they would have time with him. I slept better that evening, but still awoke several times to call the nurse and request an update on his condition. The next day, the family went in early to visit, and I stayed home to finish paying bills, and getting groceries.

It was about noon when I headed back to the hospital. As I turned the corner and started to walk down the corridor towards Ed's room, I stopped. My blood ran cold. Nancy, my sister–in–law, and her husband, Bob, stood in a circle with the pulmonologist. They stopped talking and turned to look at me. Their faces were etched with grief. I quickened my stride and came face to face with the doctor. I asked no questions. I couldn't speak.

"I'm sorry, Mrs. Williams, I'm so sorry."

Before the doctor could even begin to explain, I rushed into Ed's room. He was alive. Rushing to his bedside I took his hand and clutched it gently. He was panting, and his heart was racing.

"I'm here, my darling, I'm here."

He turned toward me. His eyes pleaded for help. There was little I could do, but to speak softly and calmly.

"Breath slowly, slowly, I'm here with you. You need to control your breathing." He never took his eyes off me as I started humming and reciting verses from songs sung by Nat King Cole. I could only remember snatches, and what words I could remember I whispered in his ear.

"Think of the first time you took me to Hawaii and we listened to the surf pounding on the shore. Slowly; breath slowly." I said. He held my hand and not once did he look away. His sister, Nancy, stood outside and said she could hear him becoming calmer with each word spoken. He concentrated and finally the panting eased. Unfortunately, later that evening he had to be intubated for the third time.

My hopes were dashed, and I could no longer think of anything. I went through each day not thinking, not hoping, just existing from day to day. I did not want to think of the inevitable.

Our four children took turns visiting. Les, our eldest

son, took a week off from work to stay with him. On his return home, he passed the car keys to his sister, Carol, and then she took over. Kimberly, our youngest was followed by our niece, Karen. A member of the family was always in the room with Ed. We didn't want to miss any of the army of physicians that came and went at various hours. The only time we left was late in the evening, and only when he was at rest. Explicit orders were given to the nurse on duty to call me if there were any changes.

In the third week of his hospitalization there seemed to be some improvement. The congestion in his lungs began to dissipate and once again they removed him from the ventilator. A physical therapist came in, and for the first time in weeks, Ed was helped into a sitting position. He was so weak, but his spirit was willing. Once again I could hold him in my arms as he leaned on me for support.

"You did well, Dr. Williams. I'll be in tomorrow and we'll try to have you sit up a bit longer." The therapist was encouraging.

Ed could barely talk. Each word came out garbled and he was still having difficulty breathing. That was his first therapy session and the last. It exhausted him.

I left that evening with mixed emotions. I knew that being bedridden for three weeks would weaken anyone, but I had to think positively.

The positive thinking didn't last. On November 21, 2005, Ed started panting as though he had run a marathon in record time. I felt helpless and I could not take my eyes off him or the monitors.

Toni, my daughter–in–law, stayed with me in his

room. It was a horrible scene to watch him fighting for every breath, but he could not control his breathing. I fought back the tears.

"Where is a doctor? There must be something we can do." I was frantic.

The nurse stood with us watching his heart rate 140, 145, 150, 145, 140 and back up again.

"Good God, do something, he can't take much more of this." Toni put her arms around me for support. I wanted to hold him but I couldn't. He was imprisoned in his bed. All I could do was soothe his brow.

I don't think he even knew we were there. The nurse was on the phone consulting with the doctors. She started decreasing one IV, increasing another, and then came the morphine injections. Up to this point, Ed had refused the morphine; now he had no choice. A few hours later, the medication finally kicked–in and Ed's heart rate dropped to within normal limits. He was heavily sedated, and resting peacefully.

Physically and emotionally exhausted from sitting in the cold room listening to the constant hum of the various monitors, Toni and I finally went home. I called the hospital at 2:00 a.m. the morning of November 22. The nurse told me he was resting, and they were able to control his heart rate. Unbeknownst to me, Carol, my daughter, the cardiologist, and attending nurse were in constant communication. Ed, for the moment, was critical but stable.

At 5:00 a.m. the telephone rang. I literally jumped and grabbed the telephone. Before I could answer, the head nurse said, "Mrs. Williams, do you give us permission to re–intubate your husband?'

"What? Are you going to do the angiogram?" I was confused and disoriented

"Mrs. Williams, did you hear me?"

"The doctors said if they have to re–intubate they would do an emergency angiogram."

"Mrs. Williams, do you or do you not want to help save your husband's life?" Her voice was sharp and cut through me like a knife.

"Yes, yes," I screamed. "Oh Lord, why didn't they call sooner? Why did they wait till now? I should never have left." I jumped from my bed and dressed as quickly as I could. The entire household heard the phone ring and my screams. They, too, were dressing and gathered around to hear what was discussed. Bob offered to drive. I chewed my knuckles. I didn't know what to do or expect. At the hospital I jumped out of the car almost before it stopped.

As I reached the door to Ed's room, I saw two men in blue. One was on the bed, the other on the floor removing the side rails. They stood aside as I approached. I grabbed Ed's hand. He was gone.

I climbed onto the bed and lay next to him. I touched his face and ran my finger over his eyebrows and down his nose, as I often did when he lay beside me. I talked, but can't remember what I said. I don't know how long we lingered in his room, but I remember the long, long, walk down the corridor that I had walked so many times over the past twenty–two days. My footsteps seemed to echo louder and louder. I looked neither to the left nor the right. I was a shell, an empty, lonely shell of a woman. Part of me died that morning, leaving a void that I knew would, or could, never be filled.

Smile Though Your Heart Is Breaking

In the days following Ed's death our entire family was in a state of mourning, yet we tried carrying on as though Ed was still with us. We prepared for Thanksgiving Day, keeping busy and constantly reminiscing about the past.

I don't know how I got through Thanksgiving. I prepared the meal and kept moving. I suppose after so many years of caring for a large family, I was on automatic pilot.

Unfortunately, the mortuary could not get a permit to bury Ed because the Federal buildings were closed for the holiday weekend. So we had to postpone the funeral until December 5th. Ed's mother and family had to leave and a private viewing was held for them to say their last farewells before flying back home to Erie.

The next time I saw Ed was in the funeral home. He looked so handsome in his blue suit. He looked younger and at peace. Nancy said, "It looks like he's got a smirk on his face. How did they do that? He *is* smirking."

The family gathered around his coffin and admired

how nice he looked. We speculated: why the smirk? What was he thinking? Nancy said he was probably feeling sorry for us.

I couldn't take my eyes off of him. I remarked that he looked as he had before his strokes. "He looks so handsome, but pale. Ed always had such rosy cheeks." Ed was probably thinking, *There she goes again, inspecting me from head to toe.* I loved fussing over him, and although he acted as though he was annoyed, I knew he wasn't.

Les came into the viewing room with his wife, Toni, and their children, Chloe and Jacob. Jacob had already attended three funerals, first his maternal grandmother, then my mother's funeral, and now his grandfather's. Ed's mother, and Nancy and Bob said their final farewells and left with Les for the airport, and I was sorry to see them go.

The rest of us sat around in the room quietly conversing, waiting for Les to return. Jacob was leaning against his mother and began to fidget. I couldn't take my eyes off that child. I suspected, that I knew, intuitively, what he was going to do. I watched as he left his mother's side and approached the casket. Reaching into his pants pocket he took out a little truck and started rolling it along the edge of the coffin. He had such a serious look on his face. His blond hair, with the little shark–fin cowlick always makes me smile. It reminds me of the little yellow duck every child plays with in a bathtub. Jacob leaned his left elbow on the rim of the coffin, resting his cheek on his curled–up knuckles. He was whispering so no one could hear. I had seen him do this once before at my mother's funeral two years earlier. He had taken a little red truck with him to the services and stood by my mother's coffin talking to her as though she were only asleep. "Granny, I'm going to miss you. Grandma bought me this little fire engine; it's red." He kept sliding it over the edge of her coffin and then he looked around to see if anyone was watching him. Convinced that no one was looking, he tucked the truck under the silk coverlet. "Sleep well, Granny. I'll miss you. Sleep well Granny." He was only five years old.

Jacob, now seven, was saying his private farewell to his grandfather. He looked over and noticed me watching him. He mumbled solemnly, "Do you think Grandpa would like one of my toy cars?" His blue eyes were glistening with tears.

"I think Grandpa would be very happy to have one of your cars. Your grandpa never had very many toys when he was a little boy." I watched as he once again slid one of his favorite cars under the lid of the casket. I felt the depth of his sorrow and yet he filled my heart in a way words can never describe. Rather than focusing on my own sorrow, I focused on my children's and their children's sorrow.

We lingered a little longer, but too soon it was time to go. There was still much to do in making the funeral arrangements. I wanted each of our children to have a part in making all of the final decisions. Carol, Robert, Kathleen, and Les helped select the graveside, and funeral announcements. I picked out his clothing, watch and rings. During the time we sat in one of the private offices at the mortuary, Les handed me a little box with some of Ed's jewelry. When Carol saw Ed's wedding ring in the box, she jumped out of her chair and ran from the room. Les went after her. On his return, he said, "Mom, Carol got upset when she saw his wedding and school rings. You can't leave them on Ed. She's outside crying."

"Oh, Les, she's right, I'm not thinking. My mind is numb. Ed enjoyed wearing those rings. I never gave it any thought. I have another set of rings we can use. I'll keep these. I'm so glad you told me."

Carol later told me that she always saw photos of him wearing those two particular rings.

"I don't know what came over me," she said, "but I couldn't bear the idea of never seeing those rings again."

"I didn't think, Carol, I just didn't think. We had those matching lapis rings made for us when we were married. I didn't want a diamond. I couldn't wear mine anymore because of my arthritis and then someone stole it. No, I'll keep his rings. I had another set made up for him when he graduated from La Verne University. We can put that set on his fingers."

Planning the funeral with the family helped me over the hurdles and kept me on an even keel. Each day there were so many hurdles to conquer, one equally as painful as the others.

Kimberly helped with the eulogy. We actually had a wonderful time thinking of the funny things he had done. We laughed; yet tears rolled down our cheeks.

We remembered when he and the office staff painted the building. Karen, Gail and Sandra couldn't keep from snickering. Ed had stripped down to his underwear and put on one of those cloth–like coveralls, a Tilly hat, sunglasses, and plastic gloves. The guys over at

Sherman–Williams Paint Supply Store couldn't believe that his office staff wanted to help him paint. The funny thing was that the girls could see right through the suit and there wasn't much left to their imagination. I could hardly tell the story without convulsing with laughter.

Kim became rather silent and sadly said, "Dad always liked Sandra. Sometimes, I would get upset with him because he always talked about how dedicated she was to her studies. I knew he wanted me to be more like her."

"You were struggling with your own demons at that time, but look at you now. Kim, he loved you dearly. Sometimes, I was so angry with him because he spoiled you rotten. Let's just say you're a late bloomer and we were both very proud of you."

I asked the boys if they would do the eulogy, but they said they couldn't. I thought I would like to ask my friend, Mary, if she would do us the honor of delivering the eulogy. Mary was pleased and asked, "Would you mind if I added some of my own experiences and observations of Ed?"

"Of course not, he enjoyed his talks with you. He probably felt he could communicate with you on a far more intellectual level then I could offer. I really think he missed his medical meetings and discussions he had with his colleagues. He never said he did, and I thought that probably it was because he felt inhibited by his strokes."

He always gravitated towards people with whom he felt comfortable. Not having to be on guard, no airs, no pretenses, he could just be Ed. I, too, felt the same way.

When Mary asked if she could share some of her

experiences with my husband, I knew I had made the right decision. I also realized that each member of our family would probably want to openly share their memories.

This feeling was reinforced when my granddaughter, Emily, showed me a booklet she had made. It was entitled "In Memory of Dr. Edward Williams." It was tied at the top with a yellow ribbon. A photo of her grandfather was on the cover. Each chapter was illustrated with what she felt was important to him. The first chapter was a sketch of books, coded with the Dewey Decimal system, followed by chapters on jellybeans, musical notes, and lastly, a Christmas tree. Within the chapters she wrote how much he loved to read and could answer any questions she asked of him. Emily remembered how he would pick through the jellybeans for his favorite flavor. He taught her to dance the rumba and swing, and would sing, "Put your shoes on Emily, don't you know you're in the city," every time they left to go home. Emily remembered the plastic singing Poinsettia plant that wiggled and repeated Christmas songs, and that he would sing along.

Simple everyday experiences were of more value to her than anything money could buy. She ended her booklet of memories by writing, "In honor of Dr. Edward Williams. Let us all remember his cheerful actions and kind deeds. If only all of the good things in life lasted longer than they do. With all of my love, Emily."

I cried when I read what she had written. I could envision Ed dancing with his granddaughters and singing silly songs. It brought back many happy memories. Pulling her close to me, I hugged her tightly, and caressed her long dark curls; I thanked her for writing such a beautiful story.

"Emmy, would you read that at his funeral service? Do you think you could? Only if you want to. I think he would be so pleased."

"I can do it, Grandma." She hugged me back and we both cried.

"Let's keep it a secret and surprise your parents. I'll ask Chloe and Kari to see if they would like to read or say something about their grandfather."

Chloe, also thirteen, wrote a letter about how her grandfather was the only one to listen to her jokes and then he would give a silly laugh. Chloe reciprocated, as she was the only one who laughed at his jokes, while the rest of us groaned. She too wrote, "I will miss you, Grandpa."

Both girls read their private letters at the funeral services; not once did they falter. Their parents were stunned that both teenagers had the courage and determination to let everyone know what a wonderful grandfather they had.

"Mom, why didn't you tell me?" Carol was shocked. "It's just as well you didn't, because I would have worried about Emily not being able to go through with it." Carol was so proud of her daughter.

The two little boys, Jacob, seven, and Michael, eight, were upset.

"Why couldn't we say something Grandma? We would have said something."

"I'm sorry, I thought it would be too sad for you, but you know you have a very important job to do.

Remember what you did at Granny's funeral?" I could see the lights go on in their little brains. They knew exactly what I meant.

When it was time to move Ed's casket to the graveside, both little boys elbowed their way in between the pallbearer–fathers causing them to do a quick step to avoid stumbling. My heart overflowed with emotion as I watched my little boys place their hands on the casket guiding it to their grandfather's final resting place, just as they had done for their great grandmother two years earlier.

During this difficult time, I could barely cry. I remember my mother telling me, "When your father was dying, I had tears, but I couldn't cry. My pain was too great, all I could do was pray. I pleaded with the Lord to take him home and stop his suffering." I remembered hearing Mother pleading with God at the window in the hospital room. Now I know what she meant.

I recently read that the act of not crying is a form of deep depression, and crying is like opening a pressure valve to facilitate the healing of pain associated with grief. I don't know where I read it, but it is so true.

There were times I tried in vain to hold back tears that flowed dripping down my neck, drenching the collar of my dress. The tears were not only for the sorrow I felt, but also for the joy of being blessed with a wonderful family. My grandchildren shared their grief not in tears, but by words and actions. They were strong, sincere, and I needed to follow their lead. I had to be strong. I knew my time would come when I would not be able to hold back the tears, or the heart–wrenching sobs.

Our daughter Kimberly arranged for a military service. Ed's casket was covered with the American flag. A small bouquet of red roses was placed inside the lid. Small photos, letters and notes were placed discreetly beneath the silk coverlet. A small, leather–bound book of Shakespeare's poems was placed in Ed's hands. Les took Ed's small radio and placed it under the pillow. Ed loved to listen to Talk Radio. It drove me crazy. Often he had three radios playing all at one time, in different rooms of course. He said it was easier than carrying one around.

We laughed as we watched Les remove the batteries. "Can you imagine what might happen if I left the batteries in? What if the radio came on in the middle of the night and someone heard Rush Limbaugh spouting off."

I remembered that it had happened. "Les don't think it can't happen. We were flying home and Ed placed a radio in the carry–on bag. I kept hearing something buzzing, but couldn't figure out where it was coming from until Ed took down the bag from the storage bin. The load had shifted and pushed the 'on' button. That was before 9/11." I watched as my son placed the radio in the coffin. It was his way of relieving some of his sorrow. A token of what was important to Ed and to each of his family was buried with him. I placed a small silk packet of a lock of hair from each child and from our parents beneath his head. We will always be with him and he with us.

When the services were over we invited everyone to come to our home. I had made arrangements for a friend to stay at the house to greet the caterer so that everything would be ready when the guests arrived.

The mood was cheerful and uplifting. This would be a celebration of Ed's life. I kept myself busy mixing and mingling with guests, making certain everyone had something to eat and drink. Kimberly, Robert, and his wife Kathy, Kari my granddaughter, and my niece Karen huddled in a corner while Carol was busy meeting and greeting guests as they arrived. Les went off by himself into another room. The little boys did whatever little boys do. I was surprised to see old patients who had flown in from California to pay their respects. Even our janitor and former housekeeper, Lillian, and her sister drove in for the day. Our new neighbors and friends, not only came to sit with us at the hospital, but also joined us for the services.

My children said, "Mom, we were so upset when you both decided to move to Nevada, but since we have met so many of your friends, we see that you did the right thing." Floral tributes came from patients, colleagues, family and friends from all over the United States as well as from Canada. He was a much–loved man.

During his lengthy hospitalization and funeral, I was like a wind–up toy, making all the motions of living. After the funeral most of the family returned home but promised to come back for Christmas. Yes, Thanksgiving was over, but now Christmas was only days away. Ed loved holidays and always made the most of them. Will holidays ever be the same without Ed? I doubted it, but I vowed I would try. Ed's spirit would keep me going.

I Can't Bring You
Roses Any More

I have no idea how I survived Thanksgiving. Ed was not there waiting for me to take out the turkey. He could hardly wait to take a taste, even at the risk of burning his fingers. On Christmas Eve the house filled with all of our children and their children. Everyone talked, conversations were flying across the room, children were shaking packages, and I was, thankfully, preoccupied with getting dinner on the table.

During Ed's lengthy hospitalization, my two daughters had taken me shopping. It was a one–stop shopping venture. All of the men in my life received Ugh slippers, and I had already purchased the girls gifts well before November. Our gift exchange was cheerful, but a subtle pall hung over my home. All of us were trying not to think of our loss.

Before my children went home, I still had one of the hardest tasks ahead. I wanted to ask my family to go through their father's belongings. When I told them what I wanted them to do, they became silent and uncomfortable with the task at hand. I almost had to beg the children to go through his things and take what they wanted. It was equally difficult for them, but they knew it was far more difficult for me. I kept his thick Scottish wool sweater, worn slippers, Velcro sneakers, along with his crazy hats, like the cheese wedge from Wisconsin, and a jester's hat equipped with lights. Ed was a kid at heart. He once told me he couldn't recall having toys, except for a bicycle he had purchased at a garage sale for eleven dollars. So as an adult he made sure there were gadgets everywhere; duplicate sets of tools, beautiful fountain pens; a bag full of cheap knock off designer watches; books, lots of books, not to mention a collection of guns and rifles. I thought the boys would take the guns, but their wives were not enthused about having them in their homes.

Finally, the children selected what was important to them. What was left, I eventually packed and gave to the Disabled Vets. At least I knew his things would be put to good use.

The morning I put several bundles on the driveway, no sooner had I put out the last bundle when it began to drizzle. The thought of Ed's possessions out on the street in the wet and cold was disturbing. I began to double–bag everything. Not only was I distressed to see his possessions on our driveway, I actually stood guard until the huge van pulled into the driveway. I watched as the truck was loaded and heard the metallic clang of the heavy metal door as it slammed shut. As the truck pulled away, I collapsed to my knees. Wrapping my arms around myself, I began rocking back and forth. My throat and chest tightened until they choked me and I could barely breath. Finally, I moaned like a wounded animal gasping its last breath. I don't recall what happened or how I got back in the house; somehow or other I just did.

Hopefully, none of my neighbors saw my emotional breakdown, but if they had, I will never know. Maybe they were aware, but they were compassionately discreet and allowed me the privacy. For that I will be eternally grateful because I was a pathetic sight.

Not long after disposing of much of Ed's stuff, I was invited to a neighborhood event and approached by several people offering their condolences. I thanked them for their concerns and turned the conversation into something more pleasant. I did not want to dwell on my loss. It was a party, a time to socialize and forget our troubles. I was successful for the moment until one woman, someone I really didn't know, began to question me.

"How are you doing? Are you managing okay?" She leaned in closer, "I'm so sorry for your loss, it must be difficult?"

Oh no, not again, I just wish people would stop dwelling on Ed's passing. Finally, I had the courage to ask her to stop. "Thank you for your concern. I really appreciate your comments, but I would rather not talk about it because, if we do, I'll start crying again and I don't want to do that." I put my hand on her shoulder and gave her a weak smile.

A moment of silence passed between us. She looked up at me, since she was a tiny individual, and asked, "What did you do with his things?"

You could have knocked me over with a feather, but I told her exactly what I had done. I don't know why I did, but I did.

Her response, by this time wasn't what I wanted to hear, "Well isn't that too soon?" I was becoming agitated by her persistent questioning.

"No, for me it wasn't. There is no right or wrong time." I should have told her it was none of her business. I excused myself and went over to another group of neighbors. I felt the safety in numbers. I am now kicking myself and should have asked why was it so important for her to know what I had done with Ed's things. I didn't know her, and she really didn't know me. She wasn't the only woman asking that question. One of my former friends with whom I had not spoken in forty years, asked me exactly the same question. I promised myself that the next person who asked would get a surprise question and not an answer.

The holiday celebrations were over. For the time being there would be no diversions to which I could look forward. For the first time in my life I would be left alone. Everyone would be getting back into the work mode, including me. I had to rearrange drawers and closets, cancel subscriptions, pay bills, stock the pantry and refrigerator. I seldom went to the market since Ed retired. Every other day he would run errands, wash and refuel my car, and shop. He loved shopping. I would give him a grocery list including brand names. If he couldn't find the right brand, he would substitute three other brands. He would even have a clerk help him search. The pantry and refrigerator was always overloaded.

This would be my first trip to the market. I dreaded the thought, but what choice did I have? I tried keeping my composure. The first aisle I went to had a selection of bouquets of white roses and pink Asian lilies. I was doing okay until I got to the cash register. That's where I broke down and started weeping. The cashier asked me what was wrong.

Trying to fight back the tears, I whimpered, "My husband died and he always bought me roses. Now it's my turn."

She came out from behind the cash register and started telling me about how she felt after her husband died twelve years ago. The more she talked the more I cried. I asked her to stop, but she didn't. She totally disregarded the customers standing in line behind me. The strange thing was that not one soul made any comment or objections, nor did they move to another line.

I fumbled through my wallet to pay, while she continued to console me. Finally I said, "Please, please stop, I have to go." I ran out of the market crying like a baby. Everyone seemed to think I was stoic and handled Ed's death well. Up until this point, the reality of my loss hadn't registered with me. I wondered if this was going to happen to me every time I bought flowers. I supposed that time would tell.

I told my children about my experience in the market. The children encouraged me to visit. One morning Carol called, "Mom, why don't you come to California for a few days? Michael's school has a Grandparents Day. You could spend a few days with Les and his family and then with us."

"That would be nice. Yes, I'd like that." I knew that if I stayed alone for any length of time, I would just get more depressed.

A week later, I flew to California. I went to Michael's

concert and visited his classroom. Michael was happy to show me around his room and point out the poster he'd made. He had written about his grandfather and pasted some photos on a large poster–board. My heart was in my mouth and I began choking up. I went off into a corner, wiping away tears. Michael became upset, and went to his mother. He thought he had hurt my feelings.

Carol came up behind me, "Are you okay? Michael is worried he upset you."

"Michael didn't upset me. I'm so pleased and touched by what he's written. I'm not crying because I'm upset." I walked over to Michael and gave him a hug, telling him, "These are happy tears. Michael when you take down the poster, may I have it?" Michael shyly nodded allowing me to continue hugging him in front of his classmates. Michael is a little boy of few words, but he expresses his deeper emotions with the written word. Shortly after Grandparents Day his teacher asked each student to write about something that happened to them that was extraordinary. I thought that was rather a large word for a first grader.

A few days later my phone rang about dinnertime. It was Carol and she was excited.

"Mom, I just got a call from Michael's teacher. She said that when she asked Michael to come forward and read what he had written using the word "extraordinary," he went to the front of the class, but turned to his teacher and said, "I can't read it."

"Why, Michael?" the teacher asked.

"Because the only extraordinary thing that happened to me was that my grandfather died." He started crying and his teacher took him outside to console him.

The teacher then told Carol that tears welled up in her eyes also as the two sat outside the classroom sharing their grief. "Michael I understand how you feel. I feel the same way you do because I lost my father. He died about the same time as your grandfather."

I could tell Carol was awed by her son and wanted to share the story with me. I started crying, "Michael has such a tender heart. I still have the little poster he made about how his grandpa likes to read. You know, Carol, everyone thinks I'm so strong in dealing with losing Ed, but it's my grandchildren that keep me going. They're my backbone. I'm so grateful that they have nothing but fond memories of their grandfather. I know that when you were all younger, all four of you put us through hell, and there were times the lot of you didn't like us very much. Kim even thought we were a dysfunctional family. There were times I thought so, too, but not now … not now. I guess we must have done something right, because each of you turned out well, and still love each other." Carol and I hung up. I sat for the longest time drinking in all that had passed, marveling at how much the grandchildren loved their grandfather.

The days flew by and I realized I would be starting the year two thousand and six alone. Each week brought new emotions. I talked a lot to myself. I wasn't angry with God. I couldn't blame God for my loss.

I didn't send out Christmas cards, but I sent a letter and New Year cards to friends and family. I told them that I was thankful for the two years Ed lived in Nevada. He always looked forward to retiring and doing what he wanted to do but never really had the time or money to

81

do; until we moved to Nevada.

We traveled, but due to his previous strokes we were less adventurous. He read his books, took college courses, continued with his medical education, listened to music, and attended lectures at the Anthem Center. He loved living in this new environment and lived his dream, albeit for far too short a time.

My one regret is the fact that I was not beside him moments before his passing. That is something from which I will never recover. I kept calling the hospital checking on his condition and was assured he was resting. I only pray that after his heart stopped, he could still hear me, smell me, and be aware that I tried with all my heart to be with him. I heard that the senses are the last to leave the body. I need to believe that.

When I was with my mother during those last few moments of her life, she waited until I was out of her room before she took her last breath. Medical practitioners and caregivers have told me this often happens. Words, words, words, but I have to accept them as true.

Unraveling At Both Ends

I faced 2006, a new year, alone for the first time in my life. I went from the home of my parents into a marriage at the young age of nineteen. Before long, I was divorced, and left with three children. I remarried at the age of thirty—two.

Now at the age of sixty—eight, I wondered what I would do? How would I fill the hours of each day? My children had families of their own and needed to get on with their lives. No longer was there a need for me to cook a different meal each day. I didn't know how to cook for two people, let alone one. I always made too much. Ed would not eat leftovers; sometimes I could fool him by freezing the leftovers to serve another day, or by taking the extra food to a neighbor.

I realized I wouldn't hear the daily humming and thumping of the washer and dryer filled with mounds of wet towels, sneakers and other laundry. Ed never understood why I had to wash clothes every day. He even tried hiding his socks and t—shirts from me, but I knew where to look. The accumulations of periodicals disappeared. On trash day, I began to have a half—filled plastic bag placed at the edge of the driveway. The three large trash bins sat empty, and I wondered where all the trash had gone. As long as my family and friends surrounded me, I went through the motions of living. I could not cry. Something inside me was missing. Now they were gone and I was alone staring at walls, walking from one room into another, searching, seeking a glimmer of a shadow, or hoping to get a whiff of aftershave that still lingered on Ed's clothing. I listened for a voice that once crooned love songs in my ear.

Desperate, I played videotapes over and over just to hear his voice and watch his facial expressions smiling at me from across the room. Then the tears came, tears to help wash away the pain, and ease the sorrow that filled every fiber of my person. I sat hour after hour cocooned in his oversized bulky wool sweater trying to accept the reality and finality of death.

Since I was totally alone, I had to talk to somebody. My inner voice became that somebody.

"Snap out of it Beth, you can't go on like this. You have your life ahead of you."

"No I don't, I can't think, I get so distracted, I don't know whether I'm coming or going." I walk around in circles looking for things I'd misplaced. I couldn't concentrate. I thought I must be losing my mind.

"Stop, just stop. Think girl, think."

I tried, but I did such stupid things, and I was filled with self–doubt. I couldn't remember what bills were paid, and then to top it all off, instead of paying $35.65 for the gas bill, I paid $3,036.65. Fortunately, the utility company realized it was a mistake.

"Slow down Beth, take one step at a time. Finish what you start."

Responding, "yah, right, I never did one thing at a time. Not with a husband, four children, three dogs, two cats, and running a medical practice. How do I start now?"

I threw myself into packing up the rest of Ed's belongings, cleaning, scrubbing, polishing, anything to keep my mind on track.

One day I worked like a mad woman. I wanted everything just so. The bedspread had to hang evenly over the edge of the bed, pillows fluffed, and decorative pillows had to be precisely placed. Not one dust bunny was going to get away from me. I didn't use just the upright vacuum; no, I had a powerful portable to reach the nooks and crannies. Unable to resist the urge to carry out one vacuum, I carried both. The portable was tucked under one arm, the hose dangling over my shoulder, and somehow, I managed to carry a utility box filled with glass cleaner and polishes of every sort, as well as the upright vacuum. The hose slipped between my legs causing me to stumble but, rather than to drop at least one piece of equipment, I struggled carelessly and kept on stumbling. I was an accident waiting to happen.

The buzz of the vacuum was hypnotic as I stretched to reach the highest levels and lay on the floor to reach under beds and furniture. Once that was done, I shifted gears and attacked the carpets with my upright vacuum. I was angry and frustrated as I pushed and pulled trying to draw up crud from the carpet pile, but the vacuum stalled. Enraged at my dilemma, I was now on a mission with a vengeance.

"I've had it, you are not going to do this to me

anymore; damn… I'll fix you." I mumbled as I ran to the toolbox and took out a pair of garden sheers and box cutters. Charging back into the bedroom I fell on my hands and knees. I was cutting and slashing at the fringes of the area rug at the foot of our bed. My hands and fingers were blistered as I went from one carpet to another cutting away fringe until my hands were so numbed that I could no longer hold the scissors. The blade on the cutter had long since dulled. The only carpet to escape the mutilation was in the dining room. Exhausted by my tantrum, I leered vindictively at the carpets. "You'll never again bugger up my vacuum."

I sat on my haunches cradling the vacuum trying to pull out the threads that encircled the brushes. It wouldn't budge. I had no alternative but to try to disassemble the entire vacuum. Back to the toolbox for a philips screwdriver; but I didn't know what size, so I grabbed as many screwdrivers as I could find.

The unraveling of the carpet hit a nerve that triggered my anger. I felt as though my life had unraveled and I was fighting to keep from being sucked into an abyss of despair and self–pity. Exhausted, I finally calmed and collected my senses. I did what I set out to do and felt rather proud of my accomplishments. I repaired the vacuum and I told myself I wouldn't need to worry about fringes getting tangled in the vacuum ever again. How wrong I was.

A few months after that incident, when I was vacuuming, I didn't notice that the carpet ends were beginning to unravel and once again became entangled in the vacuum.

For a moment I sat staring at the inanimate objects.

How could this be? I thought I had taken care of the situation. I didn't perform an encore of my previous actions. I could only imagine what someone would have thought if they had witnessed my maniacal tirade. How ridiculous I must have looked. Shaking my head from side to side, I knelt down and gently tugged on the string. Slowly the brushes turned releasing the twine. Eight months had gone by since Ed passed. I suddenly realized that I was now able to laugh at my antics without crying. Although I was still struggling with my loss and tugging on the threads of my life, I couldn't allow myself to be pulled into an abyss. With a chuckle, I said, "Beth, you silly fool, what are you going to do next?"

Next time wasn't too far off. I can understand being stupid once, but not twice. Wrong again.

I was not listening to my inner voice, telling me to slow down and do one thing at a time. No, not me.

This time I was preparing some meals to place in the freezer for my daughter–in–law, Kathy, who had recently become a mother. In the process of cooking, a splotch of sauce landed on my shirt. Grumbling, I removed my shirt and took it into the laundry room and started to fill the sink while I sprayed on some spot remover. Suddenly my cooking timer went off. Tossing the shirt into the sink, I hurried back to the kitchen and removed the pot roast from the burner. The pot was hot but as I carried it over to the sink. I didn't bother to use potholders and, I burned my fingers. I turned on the faucets to let the cold water ease the pain. Impatiently, I started shaking my fingers and sucking on them to ease the pain. I placed the roast onto a cutting board, and put the Dutch oven in the sink under the still–running water to soak and dislodge the residue from the bottom. My fingertips were still burning as I started labeling baggies to package the food after it had cooled. My ears perked and I listened, trying to identify a strange but familiar sound. Click, a light bulb exploded in my head. Dropping the marker, I ran, and then slipped on a stream of water that flowed from the flooded laundry room. Water was washing up and over the sink and flowing under the washer and dryer, out into the hallway.

"You idiot." I screamed. "You forgot to turn off the water in the sink! God almighty, what a mess." Frantic, I pulled the plug, grabbed towels, clean and dirty laundry, and anything that would soak up water. Wiping down the cabinet doors, I began to remove the drawers from beneath the cabinet and set them in the garage to dry so they would not warp. Grabbing more rags from above the laundry sink, I started wiping the floor. It was then that I heard sloshing water coming from the kitchen. "Oh my God, I can't believe I did this!" It was bad enough to leave one tap running, but not two. I am thankful for double sinks in the kitchen, one of which was not plugged. Frustration permeated my mind as I feared these careless episodes might continue.

I came to the realization that my inner voice had more common sense. It wasn't enough to listen to my inner voice, I had to speak out loud to myself, "Slow down, finish what you start. Put things back where you found them. Don't lose your cool. You are not going crazy. Take one thing at a time."

I often wondered if the part of me that was missing, along with the loss of Ed, was my common sense. Had he taken it with him? Although he was a brilliant man, sometimes he lacked common sense and simple logic. He always credited me with that skill, and I credited him for his intellect. Could it be that Ed was now my inner voice guiding me into the next year and years to come? With all my heart, I hoped and wanted to believe that he was indeed watching over me.

This first year when I was alone was filled with emotions one can only experience first hand. I received emotional support from friends and family. The best support was from those who had walked in my shoes. A few widowers shared their feelings with me. One gentleman told me I was still very much married, and it would take time to recover. He said, "I miss my wife to this very day, but life goes on." He was absolutely correct. I still felt very much married. I am a Mrs. not a Ms. and I don't want to be a Miss.

Another gentleman, whom I met at a dance class, walked me out to my car and we talked about what we had gone through after losing our spouses. He told me he was a counselor in a bereavement group and wanted to offer me some sound advice. Of course, I was more than willing to listen to anyone who could help me through this first year; so we talked. The night air was cold and getting colder as we stood outside my car. Realizing he was more than willing to continue our talk, I said, "Why don't we sit in my car; both of us are shivering."

"That's a good idea. It really is getting cold out here." After I unlatched the doors, he climbed into the passenger seat. I leaned up close to the driver's door, unconciously placing distance between us.

Deep into our conversation, or should I say his

conversation, I listened as he told me of his beautiful wife, accomplished children, and his personal wealth. I couldn't get a word in edgewise. Soon the lights of the dance studio went out. It was black as pitch when the silluettes of the dance instructors walked to their cars and glanced over toward mine. Their body language was apparent as if to say what they were thinking. Ignoring us, they drove off.

"Do you realize that we've been talking for two hours? We really need to get home." Finally, I said, "I'm so cold and dead tired."

"Oh me too." He opened the door and got out. Still hanging onto the doorframe, he leaned in and said, "I have one more bit of advice to share. It really is important to take care of yourself, people have a tendency to ignore their health."

That is the first recommendation he has given me. I think he needed to talk, not give advice. After sixteen years, he's still very much married. I couldn't imagine what other tidbits he would offer.

"I appreciate any good information and advice you can give. I certainly need it," I said.

The light that lit up the interior of the car highlighted his face, and he leaned further into the car so as to give more emphasis to what he was about to say.

"Remember to take some good multivitamins." Without taking a breath he continued, "and make certain you have a bowel movement every morning. Good night and drive carefully."

I sat in silence, not knowing what to say. The door slammed and I watched him walk to his car. My mouth was open trying to formulate a response. The response came in a burst of laughter, mingled with tears. Turning the ignition key, not once, but twice, I finally gained enough control to find my way home, giggling all the way up the hill.

I never thought more of our conversation until the next day when I walked into the rehearsal room. Sergei, my instructor gave me a smug smirk, but said nothing. I couldn't help thinking about the previous night's conversation and started to giggle as I walked up to him wagging my finger. "Don't give me that little smirk. I know what you're thinking." To this very day, I still chuckle over the intimate advice. For in laughter, there is healing.

Stormy Weather

Despite my attempts at socializing without Ed, I was on a roller coaster ride. I had fears of falling into a deeper depression but somehow I managed to concentrate. Yet the most daunting issue of all was the thought of losing emotional control in public. I don't handle frustration very well, and that was exactly the challenge that stared me in the face.

There were times, usually in the morning, when I could not control my emotions. Everything seemed so difficult. For example, canceling numerous periodicals Ed had ordered and paid for in advance to the year 2008. Then I had to remove his name from our financial accounts and sell his car. By far the most heart–wrenching task was deleting his name from the deed to our new home. Each episode brought a new flood of tears.

Receiving brochures, sales pitches, job opportunities, and requests for donations to his alma mater or for dues payable to the California Medical Association, really upset me. Also recent itemized statements for the cost of medical care brought me to tears. Sometimes, I wanted to write an angry response and tell those who had provided care, "my husband is dead, let him rest in peace, you idiots." But as time went by, I learned to steel myself against these irritations and thoughtless transgressions.

Ed enjoyed his retirement years despite his illness and, for that reason alone, I gained strength knowing his dream had been realized. Every third Thursday of the month, Ed eagerly attended Don Denton's meeting at the Anthem Center "How To, Can Do Club." He sat up front listening and taping the advice given and came home repeating what was being discussed. "Beth, you have to listen to the tape. We really need to update and revise our trust and wills. Why don't we do it after Thanksgiving? For Ed, Thanksgiving never came.

Taking Ed's advice from what he had learned, and having a brief discussion with Don, prompted me to call the bank. The Trust Department gave me the name of three attorneys. The first number was a recording. *Nope that won't do.* I called the second, it was a human voice, but referred me to a recorder. *Isn't there anybody that answers the phone anymore?* Frustration was getting the better of me. *One more to go.*

"Good morning, this is the office of Mr. Christian Gianni, may I help you?" exclaimed a pleasant female voice.

Fumbling my words, "Yes, yes, I'd like to make an appointment to update my trust and will." I explained what I required and was thrilled when she said I could see Mr. Gianni the following Friday. I met with the attorney and felt very reassured that he could help me through this process.

A few months after Ed passed, I could not bring

myself to face the reality of dealing with trusts and wills. It seemed so final. I didn't feel right. I couldn't let go. I didn't want to let go.

Several months passed and I had no choice but to update our trust. I felt as though I was holding a huge eraser in my hand, slowly, methodically, erasing Ed's life's work, ambition, and the existence of the man who struggled to provide for his family. Even today, just writing about it creates a pain in my chest, causing tears to flow, clouding my eyes so that I cannot see what is being written.

I knew it had to be done, not just for my well being, but to be prepared in the event of my death. I needed to protect our assets so that I would never be a burden to our children. The children have asked for nothing, but have offered what is most important to a grieving parent: courage to go forward and seek a new life. I needed to learn to walk alone. The day that I was to receive copies of my will and the family trust from Mr. Gianni, I took my daughter, Kimberly, with me to his office. I could not do this alone. When he began to read the will, Kim and I were both struck by the fact that she was referred to as my stepdaughter. Gasping, I clutched at my blouse as though I had been struck. "Why, why is she not listed as my child?" I could see Kim was equally upset.

"Mrs. Williams, did you adopt Kimberly?" the attorney was gentle in his tone.

"No, I was a Williams, and she was born a Williams. I never thought of it. She was just a baby when she came to live with me. I don't want her to feel as though she's not my child.

"Please, I don't want to upset the two of you. This is

only a legality. It has no bearing on the distribution of the estate. She's one of the four heirs." I didn't like the legal terminology, but it was something Kim and I had to accept. Something or somebody must have guided me to bring my youngest child to sit with me during the session with the attorney.

When Kimberly's mother died, there was no will. Her maternal grandmother, Binnie, took advantage of Ed's grieving, and she took everything of value from the house, promising to save it for her grandchild. The time of returning Kimberly's inheritance never arrived. I recall Kim writing a letter to her grandmother asking to have her mother's engagement ring as a memento now that she was entering her sixteenth year.

My mother was with Kimberly when she received a box on her sixteenth birthday from her maternal grandmother. In the box was a collection of Kim's drawings, handprints, and photos of her growth. I had continued to send those photos and progress reports to Kim's grandparents. After all, she was their daughter's only child. One particular photo of Kim was taken when she was six months old. Her mother had had it framed in a beautiful sterling silver frame and mailed it to Kim's grandmother. The photo was returned minus the frame. A message was written inside a birthday card explaining that she was moving to a smaller home and had no place to keep the childhood mementos.

Kim thought it was a present and after opening the box of old photos of herself, and reading the letter, she was stunned to silence. After noticing Kim's expression of disappointment, my mother started going through the box. She soon realized it was not a gift at all, but a box of rejection. She reached over to cradle Kim in her arms and sooth her.

Her grandmother had no place for her photo, but she did have room for the silver frame. Adding insult to injury, she wrote that Kimberly was being very selfish in asking for her inheritance, "After all, Kim you don't need these things, I sold them to pay for your grandfather's medical care. You have a rich daddy." I have not forgotten her harsh words and neither has Kim. Later, when Kim's uncle found out what his mother said, he was astounded by the lie. Her grandfather had ample funds for his care and burial expenses.

Later, I received a phone call from my mother asking if we could come home early from the office. She was worried about Kim and told us of what had happened. It took years of counseling to try to heal the wound. To this day, I know Kim still carries the scar.

After her grandmother, Binnie, passed away, Kim's Aunt Deborah mailed her a few pieces of her mother's jewelry, but it was years too late to mend the hurt.

I only hope that what I did with the attorney's would ensure Kim that her brothers, her sister and I would always be there for her. We are a family, and nothing will ever change that, so help me God!

Think Twice Before You Answer

Updating my trust and will was anticlimactic compared with what I had experienced dealing with my mother's estate. I was physically and emotionally unprepared for the chaos. Never in a million years did I ever think that my mother would disown her first born, but she did. It was an issue strictly between mother and daughter, but I was the one who was going to suffer the consequences of Mother's actions.

I love my family and I had no idea how or what I was going to say to my sister, or to my niece and nephew. The fear of their thinking I had put undue influence on Mother gave me nightmares. I was already suffering from insomnia, and now this!

My mother was on a mission. There was no reasoning with her; so I had little choice but to comply with her demands. Since my mother mutilated the English language, no attorney in his or her right mind would touch this issue. I went through the phone book, but to no avail. Each one with whom I spoke refused to come to the nursing home to meet with her. Reluctantly, I made arrangements with the nursing staff, for a wheelchair, and medication Mother would need for an overnight stay in Vancouver. The long drive from Delta, B.C. to Vancouver would be very uncomfortable for her, but she had no other options open to her because of her age and language problems. Mr. Kornfeld, an attorney and a fellow Hungarian, had known my mother for years. He was the logical choice and was willing to execute a new will.

I wheeled Mother into the office of Mr. Kornfeld, and they greeted each other with the typical hugs and Hungarian blessings. I, on the other hand, could not hold my tongue and told him what I thought. "Mr. Kornfeld, I am not the least bit pleased with what my mother is doing. There is only my sister and me left to inherit what she may leave when she passes."

"Quiet, I know what I'm doing, this is not your business." Mother never minced words.

Ignoring her command, I continued pleading, hoping Mr. Kornfeld would come up with a solution to my dilemma. "There are just the two of us," I said. He listened as I explained how I felt about my mother's actions, disinheriting my older sister, Margaret, and leaving everything to me.

Turning to my mother, the attorney asked, "Mrs. Melics, does Margaret have children?"

Mother responded in Hungarian to each of his questions. She had great respect for Mr. Kornfeld, especially after he had convinced her to put her apartment into her name and not just the names of Margaret and me. He then suggested that she leave a certain percentage of her estate to my sister's two children.

Mother banged the table with her fist. "No."

Shocked at her outburst, "Mom," I said, "You love

Bobby and Karen. They have been good grandchildren. Margaret said she didn't want any of your money. Mom, please."

Finally she acquiesced, "You right. Okay." Mother continued half in Hungarian and half in broken English, and asked the attorney to write into the will why she had decided to change it. He agreed.

On the way back to the nursing home in Delta, she broke the silence between us and said, "I am so glad that I have lived long enough to change the will. Now I am ready to go."

Mother died January 5, 2004, a month after the finalization of the will. I made all the arrangements for the viewing of the body, the funeral, and reception, according to her wishes. My sister offered no help, nor did I ask for any. I could not face her and, under the pretext of being busy with funeral arrangements, I was able to avoid a confrontation. I kept her informed as to what everything was costing, especially the fourteen percent goods and service tax, that Canada Revenue demands, even after death. Each time we talked over the telephone, my stomach was in knots and I prayed for help to keep my emotions in check.

I did explain, with much difficulty, to my nephew, Robert, what their grandmother had done. All he could say was, "Granny always did get the last word." He was the one who told his mother that Granny had written her out of the will.

I dreaded the day of the funeral, but all went well. There was no confrontation. My sister accepted the fact that the will was changed, and was satisfied that at least her two children received what should have been her portion. Robert also explained to his mother that granny also had oral stipulations that I should continue to support her brother in Romania.

When I returned home, I forwarded a copy of the will, and a complete accounting of Mother's estate, along with a check, to my niece and nephew. When my sister stated she never received a copy of the will, her son told her that he had received a copy with a check. Neither child wanted their mother to read their grandmother's final statement. I was relieved.

Dealing with international law was daunting. Since I was no longer a Canadian citizen or resident, proceeds from my share of the sale of Mother's apartment was withheld until Canada Revenue was satisfied that the taxes had been paid. Canada Trust needed copies of the will, bank account numbers, and social security numbers for both my mother and me.

During this period of time, I was physically and emotionally exhausted from the anxiety of Ed's health, selling our home, which had fallen in and out of escrow, and purchasing our new home in Henderson. In addition, the due date for reimbursing my 401K from which we had borrowed the money to purchase our new home was looming on the horizon. In addition to the financial issues, I was also physically and emotionally spent from making arrangements for the packing, moving and unpacking, not to mention the flights each month to tend to my failing mother. I knew her time was nearing and I wanted to be with her. I had become irritable, easily agitated and somewhat unstable. Ed did what he could to help. He was my anchor. I could always count on my husband to guide and protect me, mostly from myself.

To finalize my mother's estate I had to fax numerous documents to the Canada Trust Company. I took all of the documents to the UPS store and, since I was next to the market, I decided to pick up a few groceries before returning home.

"Beth, did you get everything sent off to the bank?" Ed asked as he helped me unload the car, bringing in the bags of groceries.

"Of course." I said, while I unpacked and put everything away. But once the groceries were put away, I realized something was missing. "Ed, did you pick up the documents?" I began searching through the empty bags looking for the packet.

"No, I thought you brought them in."

Panic struck! I became hysterical searching through the trash bin, the car, everywhere. "Oh my God, I lost them. What did I do?"

I was a pitiful sight wailing like a Banshee. The packet of information was a thief's dream. How could I be so careless?

"I can't take anymore," I said. "I can't, I can't. I've got to go back to the market, maybe somebody found them."

"No, I'll go, you're in no condition to drive anywhere." Ed never raised his voice, and was concerned and probably disgusted with me for carrying on like a fool.

I was overwhelmed with anxiety. "I better call the bank and have them close all of the accounts." As I picked up the telephone, I heard a beep indicating there was a message waiting. For a moment, I must have been lucid, and dialed the code to receive the message.

"This is Mr. Garcia, the owner of UPS. You left a package in the shopping cart and a gentleman turned it in. Our office will open again tomorrow at 8:00 a.m." I was still holding the telephone in my hand when Ed walked in the door. I could see disappointment and frustration etched on his face. Nausea and weakness overwhelmed me. "Oh Ed, I am so sorry. I feel as though I'm going crazy. I can't think straight. I have been so irritable. I can't stand myself." Then I told him the documents had been found and we could retrieve them in the morning.

The room began to spin. I leaned on Ed, and he guided me to the sofa where I buried my head in his lap. "Am I going crazy? I've been such a bitch."

Patting me on the head calmly he said, "That's quite an understatement."

Lifting my head from his lap, I looked up at his face. He smiled and said nothing. I put my head back in his lap accepting his honest response. We sat peacefully silent for a long, long time. There was nothing else to say.

As Time Goes By

Between the storms of being a new widow there was sunshine. I weathered the legal challenges, yet there was still Internal Revenue waiting to make certain they would get their pound of flesh. I wasn't concerned about filing the tax return because there were still issues I had not addressed, but I wasn't certain what they were.

Each week I went to the cemetery and took fresh roses to my husband's grave. Usually I didn't stay very long, but one day I lingered longer than usual. It was a beautiful day as I walked around looking at different headstones, thinking of nothing in particular. After awhile, I sat down on the huge rock next to the stream by Ed's grave. I couldn't stop staring at the empty plot next to him.

A sudden flurry of activity drew my attention to a huge desert hare that skittered across the broad expanse of lawn, and burrowed deep into the lush shrubbery that edged the flowing streamlet. Birds snatched twigs to build and flitted from ground to trees. A cacophony of chirping filled the air, sounding like a family dispute on how the nest should be built. It was mesmerizing.

The carillons began to peal. It was noon and the sun

was overhead. Despite the sun's warmth, my bottom was getting cold. It was then that I realized what I wanted to do. No longer did I need to ponder over the fate that would befall my remains when I passed away.

"Do you know what, Ed? I'll be damned if I am going to let some buxom blonde be buried beside you. If there's going to be any hanky panky down there, it better be with me." I couldn't help laughing at myself.

Without hesitating, I drove up to the office and walked confidently through the doors and asked for a sales representative.

"Hello, Mrs. Williams, it's nice to see you again. What can I do for you?"

I wasn't surprised that the representative knew who I was. It wasn't long ago that I made arrangements for Ed, and discussed my being cremated and having my ashes placed in the same plot as Ed, but now I had changed my mind "Yes, there is something you could do for me. I'd like to know if the plot next to my husband is still available?"

"I believe it still is." The representative replied. "It really is a lovely spot. I know we recently sold a plot, but let me determine if the one right next to your husband is still available. Yes, yes it is. We recently sold two in that area. Are you interested in buying it?"

"Yes, I am!" I responded. Right then and there I purchased the plot, and all that goes with a burial, even the music. The only item I didn't purchase was the headstone. Bounding out of the office, I drove home as though I had planned a wedding, not my own funeral. But that is how I felt. The realization that I was not afraid to die made me feel eerily wonderful.

I sent copies of the documents to my children. Needless to say, I soon received several phone calls questioning my sanity. Convinced that I was not going mad, they accepted my decision and asked, "What do you want on the headstone, Mom?"

"All I want is one headstone joining your father and me together. Whatever the four of you choose to inscribe on the headstone will be totally up to you." Then I explained to my children that dealing with the loss of a loved one is a painful process and I wanted to make it as easy as possible for them, while reassuring them that I wasn't about to do something stupid. I was of sound mind, although at times I felt a little frazzled.

A little frazzled really didn't describe some of the oddball things I did. Everyone who has lost a spouse tells me this is quite normal and as time goes by it gets easier. My question was, "How much time." I know some people who have never gotten over their loss. Admittedly, I was feeling guilty as I felt happy and upbeat.

Some of my lady friends shared their feelings with me and even a few have exclaimed, "I can do what I want, and go where I want. I don't need someone telling me what I can or cannot do."

Yet … I still needed reassurance, some sort of approval of how I was conducting myself. I wasn't a stifled wife, but I knew the boundaries, and I still wanted to live within those boundaries.

One night I had a dream that supported these feelings. It lasted but a split second, but was paramount. Ed and I were dancing in a studio located on Tropicana Avenue in Las Vegas. As we walked out of the private room, I grabbed Ed's hands and said, "Let's try that step one more time so we won't forget."

He smiled, the dream abruptly ended, and I woke with a start. Frustrated, I tried to continue the dream by fluffing up my pillow and pulling the blankets over my head, but to no avail. It was one of the first dreams I've had of Ed since he died, and in the dream, he looked like he did before he died.

We loved to dance and I missed the way we would playfully grab each other and sway in time to the music. Some mornings, when he ambled out to the kitchen, I would embrace him and say, "dance with me."

He would for a moment and then ask, "Did you bring in the paper?"

"It's already on the table." I'd give him a little shove, playfully slapping him on the shoulder. He'd give me an impish grin and thank me.

The dream seemed to encourage me to continue dancing, but I wondered with whom and where? I had returned to our Monday night dance lessons at Anthem Center where we both practiced. Everyone was happy to see me back, but I felt awkward. There were only couples, except for me. The instructor had no choice but to dance with me. A few weeks after my return, the instructor stopped to correct another couple. Frustrated, he crudely announced, "As an instructor I shouldn't have to dance with a single. It's difficult to see what the couples are doing." I was stunned, but I held my composure and completed the sequence. At the first opportunity I excused myself under the pretext that I had a date to play table tennis. I barely made it to the car before I burst into tears. I felt as though I'd been harpooned through the heart. I wasn't about to let that happen ever again.

I took the dream as an omen to continue dancing and decided to take lessons at a private studio. Fortunately, one had opened near my home. *Just do what you have to do. At least you can get it out of your system.* Those thoughts kept running through my mind. I had to summon all of my courage to walk into the studio and take my first lesson.

The instructor was very young and I felt like an old fool, embarrassed, stiff, and distant. When I was married, I never had a problem dancing with other men, but this was different. I can't explain why I felt this way. I felt as though it was too intimate. The instructor picked up on my emotions and asked me what was wrong.

"I can't explain myself. I haven't really danced for the past two years and I am rusty. I don't know. I'll get over it, just be a little patient with me." But I knew what the problem was. Every time Ed and I danced, it felt sensual, and I had this stupid idea that I would forget where I was and get carried away, or just give out wrong signals. How silly of me, but crazy thoughts flowed through my numbed brain cells.

The weeks went by and I was getting more comfortable. I attended one or two Friday night dance parties, but I felt more alone than ever before. Each time I left quickly before I fell apart.

Over time I met several ladies, mostly widows, and we openly discussed how we felt. Many–a–time I thought, at least I am not alone. These ladies understood how I was feeling and it was cathartic, discussing our feelings about having to adjust to living the life of a single woman.

One day I received a phone call from a lady who introduced herself as Yolanda. She was a widow who liked to dance and travel. She heard about me from a mutual friend and thought we should get together. I agreed and we met for lunch.

She told me that, from time to time, she hired a dance instructor to escort her to various events, and asked if I would like to go with her and split the cost. Without hesitating, I said a little too enthusiastically, "Yes, I would like that." I couldn't believe what I had just said. Never in a million years did I ever think I would do such a thing. I called my youngest son and told him what I'd agreed to do.

"That's okay, Mom, do it, but don't take him home."

I laughed. "I think I have enough self respect to know what I'm doing."

"Let me know how it goes. I love you, Mom." He was joking with me and was assuring me that what I was about to do was okay.

My girls thought it was a fun idea. "Why not, Mom, it's better than sitting home alone. Go for it."

Yolanda picked me up and we were both elegantly gowned. My daughter, Carol, had arrived a few hours earlier to spend the night before continuing her trip from Aspen, Colorado to Corona del Mar, in California. Carol helped me into my gown and pulled up the zipper She commented on how nice Yolanda and I looked and took a photo. I felt a little giddy, but excited. This was a whole new world, and I was bursting out of a time warp. I kept thinking about the dream, reminding me it was okay. Oh, if I could only have another dream of Ed assuring me that what I was doing was okay. My emotional stability was constantly being challenged. A few months ago I had a husband to lean on, but now I was alone and missed my sounding board.

Yolanda drove to the Gold Coast Casino, just off Las Vegas Boulevard. She strode in with all the confidence in the world. I followed. We met our paid escort in the lobby of the ballroom, and after introductions, we found our table. Don loved to talk, and Yolanda was not too pleased about his chatter. She wanted to dance. This was so foreign to me that I deliberately sat out several dances. I didn't want her to get upset with me. On the way home she was still fuming, "I didn't pay him to talk." She said, "Do you know I found him out in the hallway smoking?"

"No, but I did think he was in the restroom far too long." The thought that she might not ask me to join her again ran through my mind. But she did ask me again, this time with a different escort. He was more conscientious about his dancing duties, and I didn't sit out many dances.

I really enjoyed the chance to dance and not sit like a wallflower waiting to be asked. At one gala dinner dance to which I had been invited, I tried to look like I was having a good time, but that was prior to knowing about paid escorts. During the whole evening I was asked to dance only once. The gentleman who asked me to dance was a neighbor living with his significant other. Later when she walked past, she wouldn't even look at me, although we knew each other. He walked behind her and gave me a slight shrug of his shoulders and a sheepish grin. I thought, *my word, I only danced with him, what's the big deal?* But apparently it was a big deal. My husband danced with other women and I with other men. Why was this so different? I was beginning to realize that I had a lot to learn.

The idea of sitting at home was depressing. I began to lose interest in everything. When bored, I would dabble around on the computer and play scrabble. I wasn't interested in writing, or keeping my checkbook in balance. This was not good, but I had the sense to know I had to quit feeling sorry for myself over losing Ed.

I became more involved with my writing group and I played table tennis twice a week. I became peppier and it was a little easier walking into an empty house. I was no longer looking at my watch, thinking I'd been away from home longer than I should.

One day I received a telephone call from another lady who I didn't know. She introduced herself as Joanna; she was a divorcee and wanted to attend a Singles Club get–together at Trumpets. I refused and told her that maybe later. Later finally came, and I did, but with reluctance, agreed to meet her there.

I had never seen the woman before, so we described what each would be wearing and agreed to meet at 5:15 p.m. I waited till 5:30 p.m. I was getting anxious and felt like a fish floundering on the shore. I told my friend Mary how nervous I was, and she agreed to sit at the bar to give me moral support. Boy, did I need it. At 5:45 p.m. Joanna walked in and never bothered to apologize for keeping me waiting. I let it ride, but I wasn't happy.

No sooner had she signed in and paid her dues, than she was picked up like a juicy morsel of fresh meat, and it became evident that I was a third wheel. For me, it was time to leave. I was so thankful Mary was there. She introduced me to some of her acquaintances; otherwise I would have left fighting tears of depression.

Each episode, as difficult as it was, emboldened me. I still feel uncomfortable walking alone into a room filled with people, but I do it, knowing Ed would be proud of me.

Some Enchanted Evening

Several of my neighbors invited me to their homes for family night dinners or just to come over and socialize. I can choose to be alone or to mix and mingle, it's just doing it that is difficult. As a result some of these informal gatherings were very interesting and most informative. For example, one evening when Jessica and I were out for an evening stroll, she asked if I had been invited to a lingerie and sex toy party.

"A what party?" I exclaimed, "Did I hear you right?"

"Yah," Jessica was obviously embarrassed. "I've been invited by a neighbor down the street. I tried thinking of an excuse to refuse. I finally told her I had an appointment to pick up my girlfriend from the airport."

"No, I haven't been invited. They probably think I am too much of a square. But if I were invited, I imagine rumors would spread about the merry widow. Maybe, just for the hell of it, I should invite myself. So, when is this party?" We couldn't stop laughing. I'm not a prude, and what goes on in the privacy of my neighbor's home is of no concern to me, but it did peak my curiosity.

About this same time my daughter, Carol, thought

I needed to get away, even if only for a weekend. She could sense my melancholy mood by my voice over the telephone. I tried being upbeat and positive, but I still felt that strong draw that was keeping me close to home. Carol insisted I go to New York with her and my granddaughter, Emily. I agreed to go and, therefore, I never did find out how the party went or who had been invited. I guess since I was an aging widow, they may have thought I was over the hill. I may be over the hill, but I'm not dead yet. I wasn't asked, but if I had been, I had a good excuse not to attend.

We arrived in New York City on September 10th, ready for shopping and the theatre. We stayed at Trump Towers with windows facing Central Park and Columbus Circle. Carol, Emily, and I made the most of Sunday with shopping and ended the evening by attending the stage play, 'Putnam County Spelling Bee.' The next day, Monday, was another full day of shopping on Canal Street, and climbing in and out of cubbyholes to check on the quality of knock–off designer bags. Although I was becoming exhausted by trying to keep up with my girls, I hung in there.

That night the concierge made reservations at the Terepan Restaurant for a late dinner. After a wonderful meal, Carol and Emily went off to the restroom while I waited by the front door reading a cookbook written by the chef, who happened to be Hungarian. Suddenly, I noticed a man staring at me. Trying to ignore him I continued reading and chatting with the hostess. The man stood up. He was about my age, quite tall, with wavy gray hair, and very well dressed. He closed the space between us.

"Excuse me Sir, do we know each other?" I was a little nervous and became even more so when he bowed and took hold of my left hand. I could feel myself blushing and becoming embarrassed, yet enchanted by the stranger, as he murmured in a thick Italian accent, "You, dear lady, are so elegant. You are the lady in my dreams." In true European fashion, he kissed the back of my hand. I was stunned and became a little giddy.

Carol and Emily returned in time to witness the kissing of my hand. Emily's mouth dropped open and her brilliant brown eyes almost popped out of her head. For the life of me, I can't remember what other pretty patter he offered, but I was enjoying every moment. All I could say to his two friends sitting nearby was, "He must be Italian." I almost asked, "Is he drunk?"

Carol stuttered, "Mom, I can't believe I saw someone trying to pick you up. You're my mother!" She quickly ushered me out to a waiting cab. "Emily and I are going to Virgins to get a DVD, do you want to come or do you want to be dropped off at the hotel?" The two could not stop talking about some man trying to pick me up. I didn't pay much attention to their request. It was quite obvious that I had enjoyed the romantic encounter. What woman wouldn't be thrilled, especially at my age?

"No, I'm tired just drop me off."

"Are you sure you aren't going to take the next cab back to the restaurant?" My two girls were making the most of it, while I kept grinning, thinking, *I can't believe this is happening to me. Maybe my life will move forward. I guess I'll just have to wait and see. Wow!* I have such silly pipe dreams, but so what!

The weekend in New York lifted my spirits and I

wondered on the flight back home, *will this be the one and only brief romantic overture I receive?* I hoped not. I have no intentions or illusions of remarrying, but that doesn't mean I can't enjoy a compliment.

Have I Told You
Lately That I Love You?

Quite often, several other widows, and I go to various events around town. Every time I get the opportunity, I do go and try to enjoy myself. We laugh, joke, and make fun of ourselves. We sound like a chorus when we say, "Widowhood Sucks." or "What golden years, it's more like rust." It sounds corny but that's exactly how we feel, and yet we can still make the most of our unfortunate situation. We all know it could be worse.

Angela, an enthusiastic gambler, received two tickets for the Rod Stewart concert. One evening she picked me up and we drove to the MGM Grand Hotel and checked into our room for the evening. She went off to gamble and I stayed in the room to read. We planned to meet at 7:00 p.m. next to her favorite slot machine, and then make our way to the arena.

Ten thousand people poured into the MGM's huge arena to listen to "Rod Stewart in Concert". I was pleasantly surprised to see a more well dressed, mature crowd than I had expected. Several months earlier I had attended a rock concert at the Mandalay Bay Hotel arena, but I never would have gone to a hard rock concert if it wasn't for the fact that my nephew's band, Nickleback, was performing and I wanted to see him. That experience for me was quite a culture shock. The music was deafening and I couldn't understand a word that was sung. The sound waves rattled my brain as the echoes bounced from one cell to another. It took about four hours before my hearing returned.

But this time I was in for a very enjoyable evening. The entire arena reverberated with the pounding of feet on the metal flooring, applause and cheers exploding as the performer walked onto the stage in the center of the arena. It was a sold–out event.

Rod Stewart is an awkward looking, sixty–year old man, but disarmingly charming, a real crowd pleaser. He struck me as being humble and thoughtful toward his fans who threw everything in his direction including a pair of panties. Only once did I hear the 'F' word and then it was muffled. I was captivated by his raspy voice, the phrasing and, in general, I enjoyed every song because he sounded as though he believed every word. When he sang, 'Have I Told You Lately that I Love You' it reminded me of times when Ed would sing to me while we cuddled in bed.

A trickle came down my cheek, and then another, and another. I tried dabbing at my eyes hoping to stem the river of tears, but the tissues soon disintegrated into a mass of gooey pulp. So many times I have told myself to buy some linen hankies, but I forget only to be reminded the next time I have a crying jag.

Resorting to using my sleeve to wipe my nose, I was thankful that the ten thousand pairs of eyes were riveted on the performer and not me. The lyrics were so meaningful and stirred my soul, overwhelming me with so much emotion that I wanted to run. I was fearful I would break out sobbing and make a spectacle of myself, but I stayed put.

I kept thinking, *here I go again. Just when I think I'm more in control of my emotions, a sight, a scent, a song reminds me of my loss.* I really don't enjoy feeling sorry for myself. It just happens. I try hard, real hard, constantly reminding myself of how blessed I have been and still am. I wasn't the only woman in the world who was agonizing over the loss of a spouse. I imagined how some people must have felt when they forgot to tell their spouses how much they cared, or to give compliments, or hugs for no reason at all. Then one day it's too late. I have said and done many dumb things in the past, for which I am sorry, but I feel no shame or guilt. I am thankful for what I did right. A day never passed without my telling Ed, in the exact words of the song, "Have I told you lately that I love you?"

He would nod and say, "Yes, several times."

Sixteen months after I lost the love of my life, I thought, *I'm doing okay*, despite the constant reminders pounding in my head and heart, telling me that I am no longer a pair, but a single. The books and articles I have read have all given good advice and I was beginning to absorb it. Conversations with other widows, and even divorcees, aided me in dealing with my loss. I am a reserved sort of person, and somewhat inhibited. Quite often I become aghast at the antics of recently widowed women who fall into the trap of shipboard romances, shortly after their loss. *Oh well, who am I to sit in judgment?* I think and wonder at times, *could it be that I feel a tinge of envy?*

Often I have heard other widows exclaim that at least now they can do what they want, when they want to do it. That is true, very true. I wondered if they felt burdened when they were married, *I don't believe them. I hear an emptiness in their comments.* As for me, I never felt stifled; at least I thought I wasn't. My life was full, and I wouldn't have wanted it any other way. Now I have a void in my life, and I must learn to live with it. I wonder if I will ever regain the zest for living I once had. All I can do is try.

After months of grief I began to accept opportunities to mix and mingle with both sexes. I continued with my dance lessons and joined in on Friday night dance parties. On occasion, however, I still would catch myself looking around the room for Ed. Every time I had to go out of town to a meeting, Ed would try to join me. He said that when he walked into the room, and I noticed him, my face always lit up with a broad smile. Although I still feel very much alone in a room filled with people, at least now, I no longer have the urge to run away and cry.

The other evening when I returned to my empty home from the singles Friday night mixer, I was feeling exhausted and stiff, and my back was aching. It was a beautiful evening, warm with a soft breeze rustling through the trees. The evening was too beautiful to let go of that tender feeling.

I turned on the music, went into the laundry room slipped out of my clothes, and dropped them on the floor in a rumpled heap. Grabbing a huge bath towel and turning out all of the lights, made me feel like a thief in the night as I tiptoed outside. The house on one side is vacant and my neighbor on the other side is seldom home. No other neighbors were around, nor could they see me in my backyard if they had been.

Cautiously, I dropped the towel and eased my tortured, naked body into the warm waters of my hot tub. The bubbling water soothed my aching muscles, and I slunk as low as possible below the surface, but kept my nose above the froth. I turned on the jets allowing the powerful surge of water to lift and toss me like a bobbing cork. I lowered the power and began to relax. Then I looked skyward, and marveled at the stars playing hide and seek behind jet vapor trails that zigzagged across the blue–black sky. Every now and then I heard rabbits scurrying along the fence line, seeking refuge beneath the rocks. I wondered if they sensed a predator lurking nearby ready to pounce. What were they afraid of? I wondered, but I knew the real question is what am I afraid of?

It was getting late, and I was beginning to feel a little weak and water–logged. I turned off the jets, and reached for my towel. The cool air was refreshing as I haphazardly wrapped the towel around me and went back into the house. Once inside I toweled off the chlorinated water and headed to the shower. Although I am an insomniac, I slept well that evening, renewing my energy to face more tomorrows.

The next day I realized that each hour, day, or month that passed brought on new challenges I had to face alone. How much easier those tasks were when shared with my husband. Yes, I have children with whom to discuss my personal affairs, but I don't want to become a burden to them. Often when I feel as though I need to talk, I find they are busy with their own lives, and I get the response, "Mom, I'm on the other line, I'll call you right back." It hurts, that the call on the other line is at that moment more important to them than I am. But they don't know why I'm calling, and I wonder why it upsets me so? It wouldn't hurt so much if they did remember to call me right back. They really do care about me, I know that; and eventually they do call with an explanation and apology. Maybe the day will come when I will be able to get over being put on hold.

I once heard a critique of a short story that was written by a widow. "Why should I read about your tragedies, when I have tragedies of my own? What are you doing about it?" At first, I thought it was a callous remark, and I admit I still think it is, but it raised the question in my mind, what am I going to do about my life?

If only I were younger, but I'm not, and I'm only going to get older. So I have decided to make the most of the time I have left on this earth. Quite often, I feel and act foolishly but it only makes me laugh at myself. You know the old saying: "There is no fool like an old fool." Laughing is good, and laughing at one's self is very good.

I wonder what my solutions are? There is more to life than fun and frivolity. I realize that I need to keep myself solvent and prepare for the time when I will no longer be able to function alone. People living alone are so vulnerable to all kinds of scams, and sweet–talking devils that charm their way into their lives and pocket books. I hope I have enough sense to keep my wits about me. How do I know what tomorrow will bring? I try not to fret about it, but I am aware of the potential and that's a good thing. For the most part, I will decide to take one day at a time, and tell myself that I am doing very well.

John Kennedy Saynor, an Anglican priest and bereavement counselor, wrote a "Credo" about dealing with the loss of a loved one. His words struck home, especially the last sentence, "If I am not acting like my old self, it's because I am not my old self and some days even I don't understand myself."

Every word, phrase and paragraph of his "Credo" began to be words to live by. I sent copies to my children to help them understand my emotional ebb tides. My biggest concern was: when I am gone from this earthly plane will my children and their families go their separate ways and lose the concept of family unity? I wondered which one of my four children would become the matriarch or patriarch of our expanding family. I know I have no control over that issue, but maybe as I grow older I'll be comforted by knowing the answer.

Solutions. I told myself I have to think of solutions. I was watching a travel commercial that talked about one thousand places to visit before you die. Ed and I had been to the four corners of the world and loved every minute of it. There had to be something else for me to try something I have always wanted to do but was always too inhibited to try.

I didn't have to think very long. My children were planning a surprise birthday party for my 70th, but decided to consult me about when and where to have the party. My response was "in Sun City Anthem of course, where most of my friends are. This is now my home."

My two daughters agreed, but asked that I set the date, find the place, and forward the planning information, including the menu. I objected only to putting my age on the invitation.

Kimberly said, "No, you've reached a milestone; you can't leave it off."

"Whatever you decide just do it. Surprise me. I ask only one thing, no photos in a swimsuit, or where I look like Whistler's mother, or… well you get the idea, so run with it."

A few days later, I mentioned my upcoming birthday party to Sergei, my Ukrainian dance instructor, and he suggested I surprise everyone with a dance routine. I laughed and said, "That's sounds like a lot of fun. I've never performed before because I get panic attacks. But what the heck, it's one thing I've never done and always wished that I had the courage to do."

I had two months to prepare the surprise for my children, but Sergei pulled a fast one and asked me if I had a costume for the studio's "Showcase" anniversary party.

"I have a flapper outfit that's been hanging in my closet for years, but I won't wear it at my party."

"No, not for your party, but for the "Showcase on April 6th," he explained.

Flabbergasted, I stuttered, "Showcase? What Showcase? Are you crazy? I'll panic. I won't be able to remember my left foot from my right."

Not paying the least bit of attention and acting like the dictator he is, he started up the music, walked over to me and gently took my left hand placing it in the crook of his right arm. He uttered not a word, but wore a mischievous grin as he rocked on his heels in time with the music … and then the music started. Da, da, dada da. The song from the Broadway show, Chorus Line began, "One Singular Sensation." Obediently, I followed, not taking my eyes from him for a second. My knees were weak and I fumbled the steps.

"Again, let's start from the beginning," he commented. How many times did he say, "again, from the beginning?" His patience was remarkable as well as his constant encouragement.

I became so frustrated with myself. There were times I would stamp my feet and walk over to the wall, mockingly banging my head against it.

"Just make sure you don't bang your head on the mirrors, they might crack." Sergei laughed at me.

My clowning helped relieve some of the anxiety, but it was time to get down to business. "Okay, Sergei, let's start from where we left off."

The next two months I practiced. Sergei's voice kept ringing in my ears, even in my dreams, "Chin up, knees together, point, don't point, head up, breath, shoulders down, arms out, stretch back, point those toes, kick, step kick." Despite my feeble mind and awkwardness, I was enjoying myself. After all, I was no longer a spring chicken, but was not quite ready for the stew pot. Yet just as I was really getting into the swing of things, but I developed a severe otitis media, fluid in the left ear, causing vertigo, and nausea. I don't take medication unwisely, and for the most part, I'm reluctant to use prescriptions of any kind. This time I had no choice but to pay a visit to a "Doc in the Box".

The physician checked my ear, and prescribed an antibiotic and an antihistamine for the fluid build up. He seemed like a sensible, amiable type of person. He was a physician who could easily recognize the habitual pill popper from someone sensible, and normal... like me.

"Doctor, may I ask you a favor?"

"That all depends on what you're going to ask."

"I assure you I would never ask this of you if it wasn't important. I have performance anxiety and whenever I have to go on stage to give a speech, my voice and my knees vibrate and I can't control the anxiety. My husband gave me one pill, Inderol 10 mg., and I took it a half hour before I went on stage." From previous experience, I knew that I would not sound like a vibrator. "Could I please ask for just two pills, just two?"

"Do you know that sharp shooters in the Olympics would do the exact same thing so their hands wouldn't shake," he explained. "It's one of the prescription drugs that is forbidden at the Olympics." The physician was well aware of the reaction of the vasodilator that slowed the heart rate, eliminating the shakes. I was talking to the right man.

As I was driving to the pharmacy to have the prescriptions filled, I couldn't help but recall the many times Ed tended to all of our medical care. We were all spoiled. No standing in line at the pharmacy, he always had ample samples for us. No waiting for an appointment. It didn't matter what time of day or night it was. The most difficult transition for me since my husband died had been when I had surgeries. Although, he didn't perform major surgery, his was the face I saw before I was anesthetized, and the first face smiling at me when I awoke. *Ed where are you now that I need you? You have always been there for us. Do you know that you are our hero?*

Friday at 1:30 p.m. was "D–Day". I had a practice session and it went very well. I didn't take the pill because I wanted to save it for the evening performance. I heard Ed's instructions on how to prepare for the performance, "Beth, drink plenty of water, eat a light meal, and don't forget to soak your feet." The last time I soaked my feet, I didn't have my glasses on and I poured TSP in the bucket. This time I double–checked the label and poured in a hefty amount of Epsom Salts.

There was still plenty of time before I had to leave for the party and I was getting antsy. I decided to write; that would keep my mind occupied and my digestive tract calm.

I needed a pep talk; so I called my friend, Chester. I told him about the pill. He had knowledge of it, but not for the use I intended.

"You'll do just fine. So what if you make a mistake, no one will notice. Ed will be so proud of you. Do it for him."

"Chester, I have never done this before, I don't want to look like a damn fool. I know the pill will help. I just hope I won't need Pampers."

We both laughed and made light of the situation. I needed that bit of an unbiased opinion. After my talk with Chester, I watched the Japanese version of "Shall We Dance." The dance instructor had a concerned look on her face as she muttered under her breath, "If they start off clean, all will go well." That's it! I blurted out.

The subtitles underscored what I needed to know. If all goes well at practice today, I know I will do it well at the party with or without the help of my medicinal crutch.

My stomach was in turmoil and my knees felt a bit like jelly. My fringed, flapper dress, and feathered headdress was packed, and I repaired a small tear in the long black silk gloves. Since I could not hook up my strapless bra or pull up the zipper of my blouse, I threw a shirt over my long skirt and drove over to Susannah's house.

Thank God for good neighbors. I don't know what I would have done if I hadn't called on a friend to help buckle me in and zip me up. I would have had to wear a tent. I had all of my shoe buckles changed over to snaps, because I can't see the eyes on the straps. In fact, Susannah was also struggling with her new high heels. Even before Ed became ill he had trouble buttoning the top button of his shirt. Later when he had his strokes, I purchased trousers with special hooks instead of buttons, lightweight pullovers, and special shoes that made it much easier for him to dress when I wasn't available. Now I have to think twice about what I buy.

Our third lady friend arrived and we were off to Lowe's Hotel at Lake Las Vegas. It was a balmy evening and we purposely arrived a bit early to get a table near the dance floor. I was still calm but, as the hour grew closer, I found myself pacing the floor looking for something to do, anything to keep my mind occupied. I greeted friends, and went to the rest room several times, but I avoided the buffet table and the bar.

Sergei finally announced that all performers were to change into their costumes. When I heard that, I popped my magic pill followed by a swig of water. Once again, I needed help to change. I wasn't alone in the dressing room; the other ladies who were performing were also in various stages of undress. I felt like a schoolgirl, all giddy and excited, at least for the moment. They all admired my costume and kept reassuring me that I would do just fine. They, too, were jittery, shaking their hands and feet, stretching and putting their palms flat on the floor with their rear ends high in the air. *Gosh, I wished I was that limber.* Wishful thinking on my part.

On the way back to the ballroom, I noticed several other performers were behind the bar, limbering up. I returned to my table to watch the children perform their dance routines. Their ages ranged from five to fourteen. I marveled at how well they did. I thought to myself, *if they can do it, why can't I?* Sergei came for me, and I suddenly realized my gloves were on inside out. Frantic, I yanked one of them off, but now all of the fingers of the gloves were scrunched up in little balls inside the glove. Do you know how hard it is to turn those damn gloves right side out? Sergei helped me get them back on, but two of my fingers got caught. I thought I was going to faint. I felt like a child when my mother would help guide each finger into my mittens. I don't know how he did it, by Sergei finally got all five fingers in the right slots.

We were announced. The audience stood up and began to cheer, whistle, and shout, "You can do it, Beth." I crossed my gloved fingers, returning the smile to my friends who were also keeping their fingers crossed. I kept thinking, *if I started off clean, I would be okay.*

The music started and I was on. *Well I'll be damned*

131

if I didn't do it right. At that moment, I didn't feel a thing. *Was that me out there? No, yes, it was me. I actually did it.* The crowd cheered and I felt so relieved that it was over and I had not chickened out. Dylan, a boy of twelve came over and gave me a hug.

"You did great, Mrs. Williams."

"Thank you, Dylan. You said you would say a prayer for me when you went to Mass the other day. Whatever you said, worked." I ruffled his spiky gelled hair and returned his hug. I did it and now I can cross that off of my list of fifty things I have always wanted to do but never had the courage to try.

Despite my conquest, I was emotionally spent. Every ounce of energy was drained from my body. I could hardly wait to get home and go to bed. I didn't change into my cocktail dress; therefore, I could easily unzip my costume and let it fall in a heap on the floor along with my hosiery and shoes. I took off my rings, and the earrings that were pinching my ears, carelessly tossing them into a dish by the sink. Not bothering to wash my face or put on my nightgown, I climbed into bed, but I just couldn't fall asleep. Every bone in my body ached. My toes and the calves of my legs were in spasm. Moaning with pain, I got out of bed and tried stomping and stretching to relive the pain.

Eventually the spasms ceased. But then I realized they were masking the pain in my lower back. I had no choice but to take some medication. I put on my glasses, limped into the bathroom and turned on the light. The brightness momentarily blurred my vision. I looked into the mirror blinked and tried to focus.

Startled by a strange vision, I leaned on the counter

132

to look closer before taking a few steps back. Was I imagining what I was seeing? *Is that me?* Oh, it was me all right and what a sight. There I was in my birthday suit still wearing my necklace and, of all things, I had forgotten to remove my feathered headpiece.

The pain pills finally did their job. I was able to sleep until the bedroom grew bright. I couldn't tell the time because the next morning the brightness obscured the red numbers of the time reflected on the ceiling. I fumbled and felt around the nightstand for my glasses. I could barely lift my head from the pillow. I lay there for quite a while before I forced myself to get up to check the time and have a long hot shower. I had removed my feathered headdress before I retired, but never bothered to remove my necklace.

The whole of Saturday and Easter Sunday was no better. I simply had no energy. When I walked, it was like walking through thick gooey mud. I could barely talk. All I could think was: *is this agony worth the effort for three minutes of showing off? Would I do it again? Well, maybe just once more, for old time's sake.*

To be honest with myself, I often wondered what was I doing? Why was dancing so important to me? What was I looking for? So many questions, and no answers.

I Am Changing

My children surprised me with invitations for my birthday. I mailed them, and made all of the other arrangements, such as the reservation for the facility, the music, and the special arrangements for professional dancers. I remembered how awkward I felt when I was invited to a dinner dance and watched everyone having a good time while I sat and looked on. I wasn't about to let that happen to my friends. I also kept my children apprised of the menu selection, and they heartily approved. Intuitively, I knew my kids were cooking up a surprise for me, and I for them.

My eldest son and youngest daughter arrived on Thursday to help with the final plans. I had made arrangements for a round of golf, but unfortunately, my eldest son was recovering from pulled back muscles, my son–in–law was checking on his business in and around Las Vegas, and Kimberly, my youngest daughter, had kitchen duty while I muddled my way through arranging the orchids.

Friday evening the rest of my brood arrived and stayed at a hotel down the road. It was good planning on my part because the next day all of the cousins, brothers and sisters could mingle at the pool. If they had stayed with me, I would have become nervous and agitated with all of the chatter and clutter, not to mention the need to take turns in the shower.

On Saturday my niece and her husband arrived, as did Wanda, a former employee. Fortunately, I'd made a large kettle of potato soup, and Chicken Paprika to keep them fed and out of my hair.

Susannah and Christine, two of my friends, offered to arrive early at the Revere Gulf Club to greet guests who might arrive a bit early. They were very willing to do anything for me to make this party a success. I also think they liked being needed. I felt so lucky to have such wonderful, understanding friends. We are all so different, but have one think in common, "widowhood." We often share our feelings and emotions with one another. I read my stories about being a widow to them, and I saw them nodding their approval, mouthing silent words, *"Yes, that's how I feel."* We are no strangers to each other's world.

Soon the party room filled with the voices of my family and friends. I was so proud of my children. I did not need to wonder if I was loved, I knew I was. Every fiber of my being was filled with the love for them, from the first born, to my newest granddaughter. I was so darn excited I couldn't sit down, nor could I eat. I got myself a glass of wine, and had a sip or two, then left it on some table. I think I drank a glass of water at each table. I had no idea from whose glass, but I was thirsty and nervous.

Now it was my turn to surprise my brood. *This will be harder than I thought.* Actually, I felt rather silly, but it was too late, and I had to go through with my surprise.

I changed into my flapper outfit and the coquettish feather headdress. My two grandsons took one look at me and didn't know what to think or say. They kept staring at me. They had never seen their grandmother dressed that way. Finally Jacob asked, "Why are you dressed like that Grandma?"

I told them and they gave me a special hug as I ruffled their hair.

"Are you ready, Beth?" Sergei took my hand wrapping it once again around his right arm.

When I walked into the room, I could hear the astonished voice of my son, Les, "What have they done to my mother?" The rest were speechless. I started my dance just fine, but then my foot hit a table; I barely managed to hold it together.

Once again, Sergei whispered, "We are almost done."

It was probably the worst performance I've given. It was so much more difficult performing for family, and I was relieved when it was over. As far as I was concerned, my days as a performer were over. Gigi, a lovely French friend, had no idea what to give me for my birthday. I really didn't want any gifts, but her gift was exceptional. She got up and took the microphone and said in a thick French accent, "I do this for you." She began to sing acapela my very favorite song, "La Vien Rose". I was so touched and absolutely delighted by her courage. She later told me that she was frightened and wasn't certain how to leave the spotlight. Gigi was shocked, but pleasantly surprised, when I walked over to her and lead her into a fox trot. Sometimes I do such strange things; I wonder, *what has come over me?*

The entire evening was absolutely awesome. To me, there is nothing more satisfying than entertaining guests and hearing what a wonderful time they have had.

I still don't quite understand why this party was so important to me. I cancelled a trip to Europe to have the party. I probably would never plan another party like it. I will have other parties, but not as extravagant as this one was.

Many thoughts have filtered in and out of my mind, and I think I found my answer. Ed and I enjoyed entertaining. He was always off taking care of the bar and greeting guests. I, too, was busy across the room greeting everyone and making certain everything was in order. Every once in a while, Ed and I would connect by a glance from across the room, followed by a smile, or that certain look that told the other, I love you. Yes, I yearned for that look, and somewhere in the recesses of my mind at my party, I may not have seen his smile, but I felt it.

My children were concerned that once the frivolity of the party was over and everyone had gone home, I would become melancholy. Of course, I missed the bustling around, everyone talking at one time. Once again, I was adjusting to the quiet, but the melancholy lingered.

The Shadow Of Your Smile

I don't know what possessed me to cancel my dream trip to Europe. I had always wanted to cruise from Amsterdam to Budapest. Ed and I had planned this trip for my sixty–fifth birthday. Unfortunately, illness struck and our plans were put on hold. I suppose I was afraid to go alone. Yes, I would meet other people, but who would hold my hand whenever the plane took off or landed. Can you imagine what some soul would think if I reached over and grabbed his or her hand? A cruise without Ed would never be the same. Sometimes our memories can be a prison and hold us captive for years. I needed to be surrounded by family and friends for my birthday.

While planning the party I remembered the social events I chaired while Ed was Chief–of–Staff at the hospital, as well as the time I was president of the college foundation. Plus, our home in Rolling Hills was often the chosen site for many social events. We had acres of land to park cars, and our only issue with such large gatherings was that we had a septic tank, and sometimes we worried that it might over flow, fouling the air. Guest would ask, "What's the horrid stench?"

Responding in a matter–of–fact way, Ed would say, "the oil refinery must be burning off its residue." Ed and I were relieved that we could blame it on something other than our septic tank. We promised each other that our next home would have a proper sewer system.

Memories haunt and loneliness is my constant companion. Covert overtures have been made by two gentlemen, one by my ex–husband. I blocked them as quickly as I received them. If only the gentleman who made a pass at me in New York lived here, it might have been a different story; but alas, it wasn't meant to be.

One evening Melissa and I were having a late dinner at Trumpets. We seemed to be the only two people in the restaurant; but then I heard voices coming from a table or two behind me. I turned to look.

"My waitress forgot to bring my coffee," a man said. He was sitting alone. Without a thought, I asked him to join us since we had just received our entrées.

Melissa said, "Yes, no sense eating alone."

He eagerly joined us and introduced himself. The three of us lingered over dinner and dessert. When it was time to go, he presented his card and asked if we would give him our telephone numbers. Melissa and I did. Then we all walked out together and said good night.

"Beth, I think he likes you. He's not the least bit interested in me," Melissa said.

"I don't think so. Besides he's not my type."

I never gave it another thought until I got into my car and started banging my fist against the steering wheel. "You fool. You gave him your phone number. What were you thinking? It's too late to change my number, I'll do it tomorrow." I berated myself the entire way home.

No sooner had I walked into the house than the phone rang. I checked the number and it was Adam calling. I let the phone ring several times until the answering machine kicked in. I felt guilty and somewhat ashamed of myself, so I picked up the receiver.

"Hello, Adam, I just walked in." I lied. I wasn't certain how I was going to deal with this situation.

"I wanted to thank you for inviting me over to sit with the two of you." And then came the compliments. He had a great voice and sounded sincere, but that only made me feel uncomfortable.

"Thank you, every woman loves to hear compliments," I said. I didn't know what else to say, and I didn't want to stammer, but I had to tell it like it was. "Adam, you're a very nice man. I'm a very friendly person, and if you were a woman sitting alone, I would have done the same thing." I began to stammer but I continued, "Adam, please don't take offense, but let me be honest. I'm not ready for any type of relationship. I don't know if I ever will be comfortable with the dating game. It's just too soon. Can you understand what I'm trying to say?" My heart was pounding and I was having difficulty breathing. "I've been married for so long, I'm just not comfortable being alone with a man."

There was a moment of silence.

"I understand. May I call you again? I promise I won't burn up the wires calling you constantly. Maybe we could just talk until you do get comfortable and get to know me better?"

When we hung up I was so relieved. I sat down on the recliner and held my hand to my chest. I could feel the beats slowing. I took a deep breath and hoped he wouldn't call again. He seemed sincere and I wished he had called Melissa, since they had more in common. I never mentioned the phone call to her. I hoped the subject would remain moot.

Day After Day

As each day goes by I wonder why I can't dream of Ed. I had a fantastic dream after my mother passed away; she looked beautiful, healthy and happy. That's how I wanted to see him in my dream, and maybe then I would feel better. I have even contacted psychics and they both gave me the same answer, "There is so much grief around you, he can't come through, so he tries through other sources."

I have heard from old friends, former employees, and especially my daughter–in–law, Toni, that they had dreams of Ed. The dreams they described sounded like something Ed would say or do.

Toni said that Ed wanted to apologize for the times he was too hard on Les. In her dream, she asked him if he was in heaven. He said, "No, not yet." He said that only the more saintly people are admitted first. He is still on a lower plain, but it isn't purgatory. He still has to prove his worthiness, but he was quite happy in his current surroundings. Toni has always been sensitive to the paranormal; I must admit I often had taken it with a grain of salt. But now I think I may have underestimated her abilities.

When I contacted the first psychic for a reading over the telephone the psychic told me that Ed had lung issues and he was relieved to be free of the intubation tube. He said it was extremely uncomfortable, but now he is free and suffers no more pain. The cause of his death was heart and lung trouble, and he was intubated for three weeks. She told me some other things and much of it made sense. I so wanted to believe that Ed was sending me messages.

When I discussed this with my sons, they said I was talking far too much to the psychic and I probably said just enough for her to put two and two together. The next time, I said nothing. My back problems came up. I had just had an M.R.I. I was astounded, but still skeptical. If only Ed could send a message mentioning my pet name. Then I think I would be more of a believer. I also tried going to church, but I only became more depressed.

Now I talk aloud to Ed, but there is no response. Music fills my mornings as I sit sipping coffee and watching the sunrise over the mountains. Birds flitter about, and the hummingbirds come so close that I can almost reach out and touch them. A family of quail skitters across the lawn grubbing for bugs. Papa quail sits atop his perch watching over the brood. I dare not move. I don't want to frighten them. The slightest movement sends them into hiding. Even a rabbit or two comes hopping through, munching on the grass. The neighbors get so upset with the rabbits mowing down newly planted shrubbery. A coyote has been spotted in our neighborhood leaving behind entrails of the rabbits. I do enjoy my little Garden of Eden. It is now a sanctuary and the last gift I received from my husband.

I know that this is my time and place to reflect, to cry, and to let the tears flow freely down my cheeks and drip down my neck. Each morning, ever since Ed died, I have done this. One gentleman friend called and realized I had been crying. He said, "You need to avoid letting yourself get so depressed."

My answering machine message said, "You have reached the home of Beth and Ed Williams." This same gentleman left me a message suggesting I should change it as soon as possible." *Why*, I thought. *Who does it hurt, surely not my neighbor, or a friend across the room? They have no idea what I do in the morning, and frankly, I don't care what anyone thinks.* I do ramble a lot, but this is how it is when you're a widow.

I need to get back into some type of schedule. Writing takes up some time, but I'm not always in the mood to write. I have no patience for thinking up new words to describe feelings that cannot be described. How can I explain the way I really feel? It's not like going to a doctor and having him look in a book for a diagnostic code to attach to a broken heart. It's impossible.

Oh, if only I could dream of Ed. Shortly after my mother died, I was an emotional wreck. Since my father passed away in 1976, she and I became closer than we had ever been before. She was the matriarch of the family, so wise, strong, and yet gentle and loving. When I was in my teens I thought my mother was a tough old bird, and she was. Not a day went by that I didn't telephone her in Canada. Fifty years of calling her daily, and then one day she was gone. No longer did I have a mother or father, and the recent loss of my husband made me feel as if I were falling in slow motion down a

145

deep, dank, dark, bottomless pit, never knowing when I would hit bottom.

Several months later after the fiasco with my mother's estate, I couldn't sleep. I went into the family room, turned on the television, and lay down on the sofa. I was watching a black and white film from the 1940's, starring Bette Davis and Ray Milland. There was a scene in a newspaper office in which some erroneous headline was due to be printed when Bette Davis discovered the error. She ran down the dark grey corridor to the elevator yelling for Ray Milland to hurry; the elevator was on its way up.

I fell asleep and the next thing I knew I was yelling for Ed. "Ed, Ed, hurry up the elevator door is opening." As I was about to step into the elevator, I stopped and was startled to see my mother. Everything was in shades of gray, except she was all in brilliant color, looking younger and wearing a sky blue print dress. Her skin was peaches and cream with a hint of rose in her cheeks. Her hair was brown and worn in braids wrapped like a coronet around her head. She smiled, but said nothing.

I started to scream and cry at the same time, "Ed, Ed, Mother came through, Mother came through." When I turned back she was gone and I was awake. I can't remember if I really called out loud for Ed, but the dream seemed so real. Never in my life have I had such an experience. For the rest of the day I was totally exhausted. I wasn't frightened, or sad, just spent.

I remember repeating the dream to anyone who would listen and, from that day on, I stopped my morning crying jags. The dream or visitation, as some might call it, brought me peace and I was able to let go.

146

Is dreaming of Ed too much to ask? Why can't I have just one more dream of him smiling at me, letting me know he is at peace?

Beside The Garden Wall

It was one of those mornings when a soft breeze cooled the air. The sky was blue and not a cloud was in sight. I sat sipping coffee and listening to music, on my new IPOD and Bose speakers. *Wouldn't Ed be proud of me buying a gadget he would have liked?* I was waiting for the birds to arrive and adorn the Palo Verde tree now bare of its yellow blooms. I listened to the clucking of the quail and soon I watched the chicks grubbing for bugs. *I wish I could catch one and hold one of the chicks in my hands and pet its soft feathers like I did when I was a child and we had baby chicks.* I was not anxious to go back into the house; instead I decided to cut back the dead blooms on the rose bushes. As long as I was pruning plants, and since I was going away for a week, I would give my orchids a thorough soaking in a tub of water with fish fertilizer. Since it was so much cooler outside, I left the door open.

Though the morning was perfect, I was in a blue mood. I rose early, but without any enthusiasm, to get on with my daily chores. I finally had a shower, dressed, and started changing the bed linens. *What a waste*, I thought. *I only need half the bed; I should just move to the other side.*

But I really didn't want to move to the other side of the bed, so I continued to sleep in the hollow impression that once was Ed's side. I carried out the laundry from the bedroom. Suddenly, I was startled by a strange noise. I dropped the bundle of laundry. Standing still, I surveyed the kitchen and noticed I'd forgotten to close the screen door.

Not moving, I waited to see if I could spot the source of the noise. This time I heard a fluttering. I knew it had to be a bird that had flown into the house. As I crept slowly closer to the culprit, it suddenly flew up into Ed's beer mug collection on a high shelf. My heart was in my mouth when I noticed it was a baby quail. I started crying like a baby. "Oh God, please don't let it die in my house."

Shortly before Ed died, a beautiful wild canary had flown into our kitchen window. I went out to check and see if the bird was okay. Unfortunately I didn't see the poor little critter under a leaf. Startled by what sounded like a squeaky toy, I jumped back onto the patio. My head reeled and I became nauseated. The bird may have been injured, but I had killed it. When Ed left to go to the gym, I buried the unfortunate bird in the garden. Once before when I told him about a dead bird on the patio, he shuddered, something he had never done before, so this time I said nothing.

Remembering the previous episode, I started to pray, "Don't let this happen again, oh, please dear Lord, help me." I couldn't see through the tears, but I knew I had to rescue the baby and return it to its mother. I went to the garage where I stored my cleaning supplies and pulled out a large feather duster. I had enough sense to bring in my stepladder so I could safely reach high enough to shoo the bird in the direction of the open door.

The chick wasn't cooperating and flew to the floor and hid under the sofa. *Damn*, I thought, *now what do I do?* I had no choice but to lay down on the floor and use a broom, swishing it slowly under and behind the sofa encouraging the chick to find another hiding spot. Finally it ran out and hid behind the drapes.

"I've gotcha now," I said. Cautiously, I wrapped the drape around the chick. Then I reached gently into the folds until I could feel the beat of its frightened heart. With both hands, I cupped the tiny chick and began cooing softly, "I'm not going to hurt you. Soon you'll be back with your mama; hold on little fella." I wasn't about to let the chick die of fright. At first it was chirping frantically, but it calmed down and didn't peck at me. I carried it out to the garden, where I released it far enough away from the open door so it wouldn't fly back in.

Relieved that I was able to rescue the tiny fellow, I realized that my wish had come true. I held a tiny quail in my hands. I felt the beat of its heart.

I don't know why, but it seems as though when I am diving into a sea of depression, something positive happens. So many strange things have occurred since Ed died, and I can't help but believe that somehow he's been sending me messages. I'm just having a little difficulty interpreting them.

It's Time To Say Goodbye

So, at this point in my life, I have set the following goals: to accept the positive events in my life, trying not to dwell on the "why–didn't I, what–if, or why–couldn'ts." I will put myself on a budget, and continue to travel even if I have to go by myself.

My daughter suggested a face–lift, and I am keeping that in the back of my mind. I think the only thing holding me back from having one, is that I don't want to become a subject of conversation, such as, "how much did that cost her? She must be out to catch a fellow." I asked myself, why should I care? I might even do volunteer work at the hospital or get involved with another club. I keep thinking *some of the social events need better organization, and I am good at that.*

I may not be the merriest of widows, but neither am I the most miserable. I do believe I am fairly well balanced. The most important lessons I have learned during this unwelcome journey in life is to keep going, mourn, and cry my heart out, but do it in private. Stay as healthy as possible and not let myself deteriorate physically. Dress–up, make–up as though today is the best day of my life. Trust my gut feelings, learn to laugh at myself, take one day at a time and do not let anyone take advantage of my vulnerability. I need to revel in the simple things in life because there may be a subliminal message waiting to be deciphered. Who knows? Maybe there is someone who needs someone like me, only the good Lord knows the answer. But miracles do happen and when one does, I'll know it.

I was taught in Catholic school that purgatory is between heaven and hell. I believe we make our own purgatory here on earth. I don't like living in limbo. It's difficult letting go of the past. For my own sake I must let go. It's time to say goodbye. Right now my heart is broken, but the following "Credo" keeps me sane.

Credo

*I believe grief is a process that involves a lot of
time, energy and determination. I won't "get over
it" in a hurry, so don't rush me.*
*I believe grief is intensely personal. This is my grief.
Don't tell me how I should be doing it. Don't tell me
what's right or what's wrong. I'm doing it my way,
in my time.*
*I believe grief is affecting me in many ways. I am
being affected spiritually, physically, emotionally,
socially and mentally. If I'm not acting like my old
self, it's because I'm not my old self and some days
even I don't understand myself.*
*I believe I will be affected in some way by this loss
for the rest of my life. As I get older, I will have new
insights into what this death means to me. My loved
one will continue to be part of my life and influence
me until the day I die.*
*I believe I am being changed by this process. I see life
differently. Some things that were once important to
me aren't any more. Some things I used to pay little
or no attention to are now important.*
*I think a new me is emerging, so don't be
surprised—and don't stand in the way.*

By John Kennedy Saynor

What Grandpa Meant to Me
(five years later)

Everything was special about my Grandpa. He was inspiring and selfless. I am blessed to have had him in my life and I miss him very much. Each time I think of him, I still cry.

~ Kari Elizabeth, age twenty-three

I could go to my grandfather with any question and he would be able to answer it. He was like an encyclopedia. He also enjoyed cheap toys like a singing fish that you could put on your wall. He was truly a unique individual. Let us remember his cheerful actions and kind deeds.

~ Emily Elizabeth, age seventeen

My grandfather meant so many things to me, but the things that meant the most was his courage, attitude, and bravery. He showed his courage by being happy every day. His jolly attitude spread and lifted everyone spirits. His bravery was shown when he said that he would do anything for us.

~ Michael Emilio, age thirteen

My grandpa was the type whose accomplishments inspired me to be a better person. His kind, caring personality is one that I will never forget, because the way he lovingly treated others was unique. I miss my grandpa not only because he was such an important part of my childhood, but because he taught me how to cherish family, respect myself, and love others.

~ Chloe Elise, age seventeen

Grandpa was special to me because he took me on a helicopter ride to an iceberg in Alaska. I had a good time with him. My grandpa was also special because he made really good Planter's Punch. He made me feel special when he bought a mini van that had a small seat that he named the Jake Seat. I miss my grandpa a lot.

~ Jacob Joseph, age twelve

MaryElizabeth, age four, was still in her mother's womb, and yet, on his deathbed, he prayed the baby would be born healthy to bring joy to her parents.

Elizabeth (Beth) Williams–Medhus

Elizabeth Williams–Medhus emigrated from Vancouver, B.C., Canada in 1961. The Williams family settled in Rolling Hills, California, where she worked as a medical office manager for her husband, Dr. Edward D. Williams, and later, as a freelance consultant. Beth and her husband, Ed, were actively involved with community and international philanthropic organizations. She has been honored with Resolutions from the California State Legislature and Senate, as well as a place on the "Women's Wall of Honor," at El Camino College in Torrance, California. Two years after moving to Sun City Anthem, in Henderson, Nevada, Edward died. Unable to continue writing her family memoirs, she took refuge in writing reflections of her past and her journey into widowhood.